PLACE-BASED CURRICULUM DESIGN

"What I find especially helpful in this book is the deliberate and repeated way it demonstrates what it means to transform experiences outside the classroom into meaningful 'texts' that are worthy of close examination and analysis. It also provides many examples of ways this process can lead children and youth to become the creators of knowledge rather than only its consumers. As educators we neglect this possibility at our peril and the peril of students who learn in too many classrooms to become disengaged and uninvolved. The learning experiences described here serve as an antidote to that kind of alienation."

Gregory Smith, *Lewis & Clark College, USA*

"An excellent introduction to the many curriculum projects that are available to the K–12 teacher just outside the classroom door. Drawing from a variety of approaches—from service learning, to place-based learning and integrated, thematic instruction—this book shows how extending the classroom into the community is not only possible, it's potentially transformative for both students and teachers."

Jay Roberts, *Earlham College, USA*

"A comprehensive and thought-provoking approach to engaged learning that benefits individuals and communities. Through the curriculum planning guides, insightful quotations from scholars, and eloquent narratives of practicing teachers, we see hopeful possibilities for what education and schooling could become."

Christy M. Moroye, *University of Northern Colorado, USA*

Place-based Curriculum Design provides pre-service and practicing teachers both the rationale and tools to create and integrate meaningful, place-based learning experiences for students. Practical, classroom-based curricular examples illustrate how teachers can engage the local and still be accountable to the existing demands of federal, state, and district mandates. Coverage includes:

- connecting the curriculum to students' outside-of-school lives,
- using local phenomena or issues to enhance students' understanding of discipline-based questions,
- engaging in in-depth explorations of local issues and events to create cross-disciplinary learning experiences, and
- creating units or sustained learning experiences aimed at engendering social and environmental renewal.

An online resource (www.routledge.com/9781138013469) provides supplementary materials, including curricular templates, tools for reflective practice, and additional materials for instructors and students.

Amy B. Demarest teaches standards-based curriculum design, authentic assessment, and watershed education in northern Vermont. A central theme of her work, first as a middle-grades classroom teacher and now at the university level, is to find ways to design curriculum that engages stude[...] the issues, questions, and [...] places they live (www.ourcurriculu[...]

PLACE-BASED CURRICULUM DESIGN

Exceeding Standards through Local Investigations

Amy B. Demarest

 Routledge
Taylor & Francis Group

NEW YORK AND LONDON

First published 2015
by Routledge
711 Third Avenue, New York, NY 10017

and by Routledge
2 Park Square, Milton Park, Abingdon, Oxon OX14 4RN

Routledge is an imprint of the Taylor & Francis Group, an informa business

First edition published by Routledge 2015

Library of Congress Cataloging-in-Publication Data
    Demarest, Amy B.
Place-based curriculum design : exceeding standards through local
investigations / by Amy B. Demarest.
       pages cm
    1. Curriculum planning—Social aspects. 2. Education—Curricula—
Social aspects.   3. Place-based education.   4. Community and school.
I. Title.
    LB2806.15.D46 2015
    375'.001—dc23
    2014021542

ISBN: 978-1-138-01345-2 (hbk)
ISBN: 978-1-138-01346-9 (pbk)
ISBN: 978-1-315-79519-5 (ebk)

Typeset in Bembo
by Apex CoVantage, LLC

This book is dedicated to all the teachers who pursue ways to authentically engage students in the world as it is—and might be.

CONTENTS

PREFACE

This book is about the many ways teachers organize curriculum around the significant questions students have about their world. Authentic place-based investigations—a practice that lies at the heart of place-based education—offers students opportunities to explore topics and issues that matter to them personally, to the community, and to our collective future. There is a wide spectrum of possibilities that weave together, in whatever ways teachers and students direct the work, the deep knowledge of subjects, real-life information, and authentic skills. When engaging in real problems and posing real solutions, students get a chance to glimpse their personal "place" in the world.

Turtles and High Water

Like many teachers who design curriculum based on what is nearby, my early work in the classroom was inspired by a desire to make learning more real. An amorphous goal, I was drawn to a certain hum that happened when my students got curious about things. They developed "new eyes" toward their surroundings and spent more time learning about things that mattered to them. We explored wetlands, old buildings, and historic sites and met with town planners, scientists, historians, and scuba divers. These encounters inspired me as a teacher and them as learners. I remember reading about the Seri people who lived in Baja California, Mexico. Seri youngsters grew up knowing how their ecosystem functioned and where turtles—an important food source for them—were located. *To know where the turtles are* became a refrain that described how I hoped my students could come to know and value the place where they lived. This reliance on and knowledge of local places has endured among native people, yet it remains elusive in popular culture. I treasured this awareness in my own life, being a great lover of turtles, and wanted to literally and figuratively instill this love in my students.

Now, years later, "knowing where the turtles are" remains a useful metaphor. A central premise of this book is that students should know their world intimately—and be aware of what will sustain them—now and in the future. Now, however, I believe students should experience this intimacy in relation to other issues and deeper questions. For example, if considering turtles, one might ask: *How has the turtle habitat been preserved or lost? Who made these decisions? Is the work to preserve turtles in conflict with the quality of life or cherished traditions of any group of people?* A student living in the brick, asphalt, and steel places of our inner cities might pose and pursue a different question. Although I am still tied to the natural world, I now feel empowered to ask more critical questions that position students to ask more of themselves, each other, and their communities. This book looks at the dynamics of designing curriculum based on investigations that begin with questions.

After Japan's tsunami in the spring of 2011, a tradition came to light of ancient stone markers that warned of high water marks of past floods. "The tsunami stones are warnings across generations, telling descendants to avoid the same suffering of their ancestors," said a Japanese scientist (Fackler, 2011, para. 5). Inscribed on one of the stones was the following: "High dwellings ensure the peace and happiness of our descendants" (para. 14). Just as the Seri people's knowledge of turtles ensured survival in their world, the stone markers helped some avoid the tragedy of the tsunami in Japan. As we struggle to make sense of the disruption of our global climate and social fabric, there are markers of past generations that dot our landscape but are lost to us. The markers we need for the 21st century will be built with trust and collaboration and foster the ability to ask and pursue questions, solve problems, and understand places and the systems that govern them. We need to build markers within our educational system that will preserve our communities and safeguard our futures.

Engaging the local is a term I use broadly to view ways teachers incorporate questions that matter into their curriculum in ways that can be transformational for the students *and the communities in which they live.* While this is a large undertaking, this book underlines the many ways teachers are able to create a positive forward motion toward a better society. In many cases, students solve real problems and generate new feelings of hope in the community. While my early teaching experiences were more rural, nature-based, and traditional, my current work is with teachers who find ways to incorporate community service into their academic agenda. These innovative approaches have led me to a much more fluid view of how we might design curriculum. Like the teachers I work with, I continue to be energized and surprised by the limitless possibilities that emerge when students' questions guide learning.

What Is in This Book

This book presents a close examination of the decisions teachers make while planning curriculum based on local investigations.

Part I: Place-based Education: Theory and Practice

Chapter 1 presents the theoretical background for conducting local investigations and portrays the fluid and complex nature of the work teachers do to orient the curriculum in the context of community. Chapter 2 shows how this approach works in real classrooms.

Part II: Elements of Place-based Curriculum Design: Purpose and Function

The four chapters in this section present the four curricular elements of local investigations that are present throughout this book and presented here in detail: a student's past and present experience, understanding of subjects, sense of place, and personal agency. Chapter 3 presents the contextual nature of learning and how local connections make curriculum more personally relevant and engaging. Chapter 4 addresses how specific disciplines can be presented alongside local phenomenon to deepen students' understanding. Chapter 5 examines how teachers integrate different subjects to explore the stories of local places. Chapter 6 explores a more critical approach to local investigations when students direct their own inquiry to address the more complex issues that face society. Although presented separately, the four elements overlap and merge together when teachers design curriculum based on local questions.

Part III: Planning for Local Learning: Logistics and Challenges

Chapter 7 explores the idea of "place as text" and presents the many ways that teachers and students can learn to interpret and better understand the world outside the classroom. Chapter 8 examines the curricular tools of *Understanding by Design* (Wiggins & McTighe, 1998, 2005) that offer ways to consider lesson plans, unit outlines, and assessment tools within the context of the larger goals and outcomes of local investigations.

Part IV: Moving Forward: Strategies for School Change

Chapter 9 is about how teachers can be supported in their work to ground curriculum in local places. It examines the dynamics of "forward motion" that groups of teachers, leadership, and whole schools can undertake in order for learning to happen more authentically in the context of communities.

This book gives voice to teachers who undertake place-based education in several ways. It emerges from my own practice as a classroom teacher and curriculum consultant and reflects the insights of many teachers with whom I have worked. In 2006–2007, I conducted a qualitative research project with seven teachers who have embraced this practice. Their work is profiled in the "Teacher

Portraits" as well as through specific examples and quotes used throughout the book. Other teachers with whom I work at the graduate level in curriculum classes, summer workshops, and classes designed specifically on Place-based Education are profiled with shorter portrayals of the way they approach curriculum. I also present the work of other teachers in the United States whom I have met at conferences, at site visits, or through networking.

In addition to the quotes from specific research participants, I include single phrases or expressions from different teachers that capture the spirit of this practice. These are most often used as chapter headings. Quotes from well-known published writers are found in boxes throughout the book.

Unless presenting the work of a particular teacher, I use the pronoun "she" for teachers and "he" when referring to students. Not a perfect solution, but it seemed better than constantly duplicating pronouns. In some examples, I do not specify a grade-level. I work with K–12 teachers, and my experience is that when there is a good example, teachers can usually adapt it to the age and needs of their students. When the grade level is important to understanding the example, I include it.

One of the biggest challenges in writing this book was to effectively present ways to incorporate national standards, given their changing nature. Originally, standards were used as big ideas that the teacher "unpacked" to determine assessment criteria. Recent publications of Common Core (www.corestandards.org), the new science standards (www.nextgenscience.org), and social studies standards (www.socialstudies.org) present the standards in smaller parts. While this may be more manageable and easier to align with standardized tests, it may diminish the autonomy and design possibilities for the teacher. I believe that standards can continue to drive best practices when teachers have artistic license to weave them together with authentic experiences and multiple assessment strategies. I included specific examples of standards when useful but hope they are presented in such a way as to facilitate the creative role of the teacher in the design process.

This book reflects what is happening in the United States, but it is not just for American teachers. Many exciting initiatives are happening elsewhere around the world. My hope is that this book and its online website become part of the dialogue as we share ideas and promising practices with each other.

The online resource for this book (www.routledge.com/9781138013469) provides the following additional information and resources and links to my website and blog (www.ourcurriculummatters.com):

- curricular templates,
- tools for reflective practice, and
- additional materials for instructors and students.

★★★★★★★★★★★★★★★★★★★★★★★★★★★

Can schools learn to grapple with things that really matter? Can we learn to look at the places we live in terms of the whole of things, not just turtles through a science lens or buildings through a history lens? As we create the markers we need to make our way in this complex world, I continue to be heartened by the work teachers and students are doing as they turn together toward their communities. In that turning, they reshape how others view school, what work is done, and how each day is experienced. In the process, a better answer to the question, "What is the purpose of education?" emerges.

We might still choose to learn where the turtles live. In our search to find turtles, or some other intriguing corollary, we might find ways to learn more outside of the classroom. We might meet people along the way and gain insight into how one of our students pays careful attention when interacting with others outside of school. As teachers *follow the honey*, they follow a trail that leads to the treasures of their own places and the huge untapped potential of the students they teach.

★★★★★★★★★★

References

Fackler, M. (2011, April 20). Tsunami warnings, written in stone. *The New York Times*. Retrieved January 2, 2012, from www.nytimes.com/2011/04/21/world/asia/21stones.html?pagewanted=all

Wiggins, G., & McTighe, J. (1998). *Understanding by design* (1st ed.). Alexandria, VA: Association for Supervision and Curriculum Development.

Wiggins, G., & McTighe, J. (2005). Understanding by design (2nd ed.). Alexandria, VA: Association for Supervision and Curriculum Development.

ACKNOWLEDGMENTS

There are many wonderful people whose talent, goodwill, and forward thinking have contributed to this book. I am grateful for my many investigations with teachers and students ... often learning in the river, on the mountaintop, and around the neighborhood. While I have learned from many brilliant educators in this regard, I especially want to thank Megan Camp, Jen Cirillo, Mary Dupont, Colleen Hickey, Carol Livingston, Walter Poleman, Amy Powers, Julie Silverman, Pat Straughan, Maureen Saunders, Linda Wellings, and Katie Wyndorf. At the University of Vermont, I am also grateful to have learned and taught with Penny Bishop, Cynthia Reyes, and Charlie Rathbone. Thanks to Ben Williams. Thanks to many readers, especially Matt Dubel, Sarah Bertrucci, and Christie Nold and the warm counsel of Elaine Stern, Ann Lipsitt, and Penny Gill. I am grateful for my long-standing association with City High School in Tucson, Arizona—colleagues with whom I have shared a variety of professional learning experiences. Thanks also to Rob Riordan and all the progressive educators he introduced me to at High Tech High School in California. I am grateful to Greg Smith and David Greenwood whose writings continue to deepen my understanding of the ways students can *engage the local*.

Emily Barrett, aka the "Guardian Angel," has been a wonder with all things technical, artistic, and methodical. Thank you for bringing your spectacular talents, counsel, and laugh-out-loud sense of humor to this journey.

Warm thanks to the seven research participants who are portrayed in this book. It was an honor to be in your classrooms and have so many rich conversations about teaching in the context of community. Some of these conversations continue! Thank you Jean Berthaiume, Gay Craig, Judy Elson, Sharyl Green, Ellen Temple, Anne Tewskbury-Frye, and Kate Toland. I also want to thank the many teachers who shared their work for this book: Helen Beattie, Chela Delgado, Brett Goble, Barry Guillot, Lindsey Halman, Jeff Hindes, Amy LaChance, Steven Levy Pauline Roberts, Matthew Webb, and Rachel Wood. Thanks to the teachers at the Martin Luther King Middle School in Berkeley, California. I am glad for my continued association with Matt Neckers who now teaches graphic design in Hyde Park, Vermont, and the serendipitous communication that led to his student, Thomas Brosseau, designing the cover for this book. I couldn't have dreamt up a more perfect "wrap" on this project.

I am especially grateful to the students whose work appears in these pages: Lul Abshir, Uriah Boyd, Ian Drumm, Zack Dustira, Dylan Grimm, Sierra Lindsay, Damion Mitchell, and Hazel Wazmund.

Warm thanks for images provided by Doria Anselmo/Outside the Lens project, Mary Ellen Calabrese, Brandon Cohen/High Tech High School, Sharon Danks, Kathleen Maas-Hebner/Oregon State University, Tom Moore/City High School, Prakash Patel/Prakash Patel Photography (www.prakashpatel.com), Steven Schmidt, Stonington Museum/Old Stone House Museum/Orleans County Historical Society, and Brian Williams/Sustainability Academy at Lawrence Barnes.

I have worked with many pre-service and practicing teachers who have been part of my learning journey in graduate courses, in-service, study groups, and workshops. There are instances in the text where I quote them but do not add particulars about who and where they teach. Their comments drawn from reflective journals and class discussions helped portray an aspect of the work I thought was important. They include Matt Chandler, Beth Curtis, Melissa Dion, Andrew Evans, Sandra Fary, Lissa Fox, Emily Hoyler, Corinna Hussey, Andre LaChance, Patty LaMothe, Megan Mitchell, Sarah Miller, David Parmelee, Betsy Patrick, Tina Phelps, Kelly Pierpont, Dick Pigeon, Josh Roof, Jeff Rouleau, Nicolle Schaeffer, and Dawn Weir.

Warm thanks to Naomi Silverman, Christina Chronister, and all the good folks at Routledge. I am especially grateful for the honest, insightful, and useful feedback I received during the peer-review process.

As always—thanks to my beloved husband, Fred Magdoff, still the nicest person in the world to live with, even when writing a book. Sorry it took so long. Let's go take the dogs for a walk.

PART I

Place-based Education

Theory and Practice

Local learning has come to be known as place- or community-based education, terms used to include a wide variety of intentions and practices. At the heart of this approach is the ability to structure curriculum around authentic investigations that bring students out into the community. In the pursuit of local questions, teachers and students develop partnerships with specific locales, community organizations, commercial enterprises, and individuals that provide the context for content acquisition, engaged learning, and meaningful community service.

Using local questions as the foundation of curriculum design integrates elements of a number of different educational traditions, including inquiry, standards-based curriculum design, project- and problem-based learning, and associated best practices. While this approach is not new, place-based education shares an allegiance to many things on which we have made progress. We now know more about:

- the individual nature of learning,
- ways to identify measurable outcomes in relation to intended goals,
- examining student work to ground teacher practice and steer school reform,
- what excellent work in the context of community might look like, and
- how to forge authentic partnerships between students, teachers, and community members.

Such a convergence of exemplary practices presents a transformative approach to education that engages learners as researchers, meaning-makers, and problem-solvers. The work students do is more rigorous, different, and "bigger" than the work happening in most schools and is a challenge for teachers on many levels. As one teacher put it, "The work that the students were doing got so big; it kept bumping in to regular school." When teachers use local questions to fuel their curriculum, they offer young people a vibrant context for traditional knowledge and skills, as well as enduring lessons about how to live their lives peacefully and productively in communities.

Attention to the questions that students have about their world conflicts with the traditional pattern of schooling in America. The predominant nature or "grammar" (Tyack & Tobin, 1994) of schools presents a major obstacle to students asking, exploring, and responding to questions in their local environment as a core pedagogy. Gruenewald (2003b) notes that:

> . . . the "grammar" of school reform lacks a vocabulary for place. Just as this grammar distracts our attention from democracy as a valued educational goal, it distracts us from places and their power to shape experiential, cultural, ideological, political and ecological orientations toward being in the world.
>
> *(p. 642)*

When students undertake local investigations, the pattern is not, *"Do you know x, y, or z? Yes or no?"*—with so much attention being paid to "no." The pattern is, *"What is this about? What does it mean to you? Where can we go to understand these things better?"*

These contrasting patterns are accentuated by the gross inequalities that permeate our society and are mirrored in the way American students access and experience education. In general, children in predominantly white, wealthier communities experience a higher quality of education and opportunity than poor children of color (Delpit, 2012). Yet socioeconomic factors and racial divides are not always the determining factors. Some schools with meager resources find ways to deliver a rigorous, innovative learning experience for their students, and affluent communities can fail to challenge their students in many significant ways. Furthermore, federal edicts carry contradictory expectations and affect schools differently. This contrast in teachers' realities, choices, and working conditions is part of a highly complex landscape in which to work.

It is the teacher's creative capacity to work effectively amidst these many contradictions that adds to our understanding of teachers as agents of change. Acting with what Henderson and Kesson (2004) call "curriculum wisdom," teachers "must stick our necks out in a high-minded, determined and consistent way" (p. 2). This view of a teacher's agency invites a:

> . . . new understanding of the relationship between democracy and schooling, and learning and social change. . . . [E]ducators need a new vocabulary for not only defining schools as democratic public spheres, students as informed and critically engaged citizens, but also teachers as public intellectuals.
>
> *(Giroux, 2013, p. 165)*

Teachers who undertake the creative task of designing local investigations constantly seek new ways to make learning happen, better engage their students, and help their students perform better. This becomes the new vocabulary that Gruenewald and Giroux call for, built with genuine connections, stronger relationships, and high performance. As teachers pursue the sweetness of this deeper work, it changes business as usual for themselves, their students, and the work that they do together.

TEACHER PORTRAIT #1
KATE TOLAND
HIGH SCHOOL

"The kids in my class have brand-new vertebrae!"

The first year Kate became involved in an ethnographic community inquiry, her students researched quality-of-life indicators around the world and then looked at their community. There was a wide span of topics students considered, such as access to restaurants, traffic, student drug use versus adult perceptions of student drug use, impacts of the war in Iraq, recreational opportunities for teens, and the quality of the sports teams.

As a high school social studies teacher, Kate ran three years of community research with her ninth-graders. In the third year, Kate undertook making a video with 58 ninth-graders. She worked with an ethnographer from the Vermont Folklife Center who suggested they explore diversity from a historical perspective. Teaching in a school where 18 percent of the students have recently come from another country and many other students are descendants of previous waves of Italian and French-Canadian immigrants, Kate set out to explore this diversity in a way that she hoped would build empathy and understanding. As the project unfolded, she found that students could see their own attitudes within a historical context. One of her students commented: "Wow, my prejudice is just like how they felt about the French-Canadians 100 years ago." As students conducted interviews and struggled to create a video that reflected everyone's views, they learned to listen to each other in new ways. They discovered things they felt proud of. "The kids in my class have brand-new vertebrae!" exclaimed Kate.

The film the students made was titled "Welcoming the World: Our City—Past and Present," and, as one student described it, the film told the "interesting and untold stories of our city." Talking with a group of students about whether to include a blatant expression of racism in the video, one said: "If you don't address these issues, Ms. Toland, [students] will leave your class with the same attitudes they came in with." At the first showing, a grandmother shared her realization that newcomers had it hard: "[The film] made me realize that I could have done a better job reaching out."

In imagining the "perfect" place-based moment, Kate replies: "I think that we would be talking about the elephant in the room . . . tackling the tough issues that the community hasn't been able to solve, that the adults haven't been able to solve by themselves. It introduces them to some of the conundrums of humanity."

Kate believes that authentic inquiry helps students learn to understand and deal with the world: "I think schools try to package everything like it's already done. Here is the world, this is economics, this is business, everything is in a box. But there's no easy answer. And there's not an easy answer in life . . . working through real problems introduces that in a nice way and teaches them their voice matters."

1

WHAT IS PLACE-BASED CURRICULUM DESIGN?

A teacher's craft is highly fluid and involves the abilities to make many decisions at once; creatively connect learners, ideas, and worthwhile outcomes; and model inquisitive, rigorous, and original thinking. The view of a teacher as an artist, while not a new analogy, affirms the creative capacity needed to make learning happen each day for 25, 35, or 145 other human beings under her watch.

The design of local investigations invites a wide span of practice and is associated with a more self-directed, inquiry-based, experiential pedagogy. The ability to facilitate investigations implies a skilled ability to structure learning around questions and to claim time for students to explore, experiment, and interpret. In inquiry-based learning, the teacher is a coach, problem-poser, and facilitator. If a teacher says, "My students do a lot of inquiry," she may mean that she pays a lot of attention to their questions within a structured curriculum, or she may mean that her students are designing and conducting far-reaching, self-directed investigations in the community. Inquiry—in educational parlance—is both an adjective and a noun.

In designing place-based curriculum, there is a particular complexity to orchestrating an authentic engagement with the people, places, and things outside of the classroom, while addressing curriculum standards and being responsive to the needs of each student. This book explores four aspects of teaching and learning that present themselves in authentic local investigations: the learners' experience, mastery of subject, relationship to place, and personal agency. Posed as questions, these elements reveal the breadth of complexity the teacher encounters in order to design local learning:

- How can I better relate school to my students' life experience?
- How can I help students better understand how this big idea works in the real world?

- How can I help students better understand this place?
- How can I help students better understand themselves and their possible futures?

Teachers create their own answers to these questions. The constructed pedagogical "answer" determines how she makes the many decisions involved in teaching. This is a creative journey for the teacher that involves new ideas, reading, and conversations with colleagues as well as the ongoing integration of past and present experience, personal values, and professional training. A teacher's vision, what Wells (2001) defines as "a point of reference in decision making and problem solving" (p. 16), develops from a mix of theory and practice.

However the process starts, it plays into and works through the teacher's belief about what is possible. This changes in relation to her philosophy, her perceived and real agency in the classroom, and her view of the young people she is teaching, their ways of learning, and who they might become. The teacher comes to understand these dimensions of her practice as she finds new ways to organize learning around more authentic tasks. She learns to manage, articulate, negotiate, and enact new pathways of learning. All these things merge to become the curriculum that actually gets delivered each day. When a teacher succeeds in merging all these elements into a unified approach that guides the learning and creates room for students' questions and self-direction, it can become a highly fluid undertaking.

A teacher might use a primary document from the local historical society or invite a guest speaker to class and say: "Wow, my kids were really engaged. I want to do that more!" She may observe students out in a park looking at weeds on a sidewalk and feel a new energy in her classroom when she talks about how plants grow. Or she may find herself entwined in a full-blown ethnographic study as her students gather stories from elders, create digital archives for the neighborhood, and host community events to share the information. Teachers find ways to create opportunities for content acquisition, such as better writing skills and knowledge of local history, as well as a vision of a personal future, job opportunities, and service.

As they mix together these curricular goals, they continually adapt to meet the needs of individual students. Working with the elements of curricular intentions, rather than a set definition of place-based education, underlines the creative, fluid nature of the process. "A transformative curriculum . . . is one that allows for, encourages, and develops [a] natural capacity for complex organization; and through the process of transformation the curriculum continually regenerates itself and those involved with it," according to Doll (1993, p. 87).

"You're not always sure what's going to happen next, but that's what I love."

Teachers who manage the complexity of these relationships have a commitment to honor and learn with their students, and a level of comfort with the unexpected event. As a teacher forms a vision of what engaged learning might look like, she might gain insight from Myles Horton (1990) who believed that teaching with a vision was a "two-eyed" practice:

> I like to think I have two-eyes that I don't have to use the same way . . . . I try to see with one eye where . . . people are. . . . If I can get hold of that, this is where I start. So I look at them with my other eye and say to myself, how do I start moving them from where they perceive themselves to be, to where I know they can be.
>
> *(pp. 131–132)*

Or she may come to see the challenge in the way that Kate Toland (see "Teacher Portrait #1") reflects:

> There are things that I can predict that the students will be able to do. But there is a deeper thing that happens—*that's the piece that's so powerful. So we create the conditions for X, Y, Z;* you still have a unit that is designed to show your principal or your school board, but you invite them to the final event too [to see] the other outcomes that you can't necessarily plan for—but you have in mind the whole time.

Teachers come to understand many ideas and practices to hone their craft. In the process, a teacher gains agency to resolve what, in professional dialogue with teachers, I refer to as the "wannas and gottas." You do what you are ready for, able to, believe in, have to, and feel is best for your students. "It's not easy," says one teacher. "You have to do what the district wants, but you also have to do what you want—what you think is important. It is hard to resolve these two."

Vito Perrone (1998) suggests that a deeper knowledge of the traditions of educational thought make teachers better able to resolve these conflicts.

> Maintaining better connections with this history, making it part of our ongoing reflection about teaching, learning and schools, keeps the dignity of teaching and its broader social context within our gaze, providing us with larger sets of possibilities for our practice, leading us to a more discriminating stance about what is often put forward as reform.
>
> *(p. 1)*

This chapter identifies key philosophical threads that teachers draw from that provide a backdrop to this practice and illustrate its breadth and possibilities.

"A Sense of Place" as a Curricular Intention

> "As centers of experience, places teach us and shape our identities and relationships."
>
> *David Greenwood (2013, p. 93)*

At the foundation of this practice is the assumption that each of us has a relationship with the places where we live and that these places shape *who* we are and *how* we see our life. The ability to listen and pay attention to one's place is referred to as having a "sense of place" (Feld & Basso, 1996b).

From an environmental point of view, a sense of place reflects value placed on natural spaces and suggests that the environment can be a source for understanding our relationship with nature. Environmentalists link this sense of place to the ability to care for the natural environment—and by extension, the planet. From this perspective, having a "sense of place" implies an ability to care for one's surroundings: Demonstrating *responsible behavior* toward one's landscape (Chawla, 1998), *ecological literacy* (Orr, 1992), and *living well* in a community (Haas & Nachtigal, 1998).

From a more critical view of place, the primacy of natural spaces is questioned, and the idea that we all learn in and from our spaces—built or natural—comes to the forefront. In this view, it is not only our ecological footprint that is considered but also the way in which we inhabit our spaces with respect to each other. Greenwood (2013) writes: "A theory of place that is concerned with the quality of human-world relationships first acknowledges that places themselves have something to say. Human beings, in other words, must learn to listen. . . ." (p. 98).

The breadth of ways in which we can understand a place is enhanced by this idea that places hold stories. A storied landscape invites one to explore and interpret and, ultimately, to take away one's own personal meaning. A teacher might consider the different stories from a number of perspectives, some of which are more straightforward than others. She might think of the stories as subject-based (i.e., the history story, the geology story, etc.) or seek to uncover the "hidden stories" of violence, genocide, or cultural oppression in a place that have been silenced over time. In a modernist sense, the dialogue about one's "sense of place" is less in "broad philosophical or humanistic terms" and more about "sites of power struggles or about displacement as histories of annexation, absorption and resistance" (Feld & Basso, 1996a, p. 5). Others may argue that the distinction of "natural" and "built" is a misleading distinction since humans are also "natural" so that what they create is also. However they are defined, places hold many different stories.

Places offer a wide span of questions that can help ground and inform an inhabitant. Questions such as "Who am I?", "Where do I come from?", or "What is my relationship with others and the community in which I live?" can foster self-awareness. Other questions such as "What was here where this building now is?", "Where does water flow?", or "Who lives here?" can develop a knowledge of place. More complex questions about equity and social justice can lead to increased awareness and civic engagement. All provide fodder for a teacher to deepen a student's connection to the place he lives.

Attention to Students' Local Knowledge and Ways of Knowing

> "[Teachers'] learning lies in their seeking to become involved in the students' curiosity and in the paths and streams it takes them through."
>
> *Paulo Friere (1998b, p. 17)*

For many students, formal schooling is about the stories of other people. Many students experience the knowledge addressed in schools as someone else's (Kozol, 2005). Books and materials describe a world apart that tells of another story in some other place. Sometimes these disconnections are blatant along the lines of race, social class, and cultural background. However, just as insidiously, the curriculum fails to make a human connection—to reach across preconceptions and life experiences to link up to a story line in all of us. Authentic questions cast a hook that asks, *What does this story mean to you?*

"Their 'place' is where they are at."

Raising authentic questions is not just geographically local, it is local emotionally. One teacher commented: "I take the term 'place-based' literally. It reminds us we always need to reach out and teach to where kids are, not stay in our place—we need to go to theirs." By believing in the ways that students' questions can guide learning, teachers turn toward students' background, knowledge and experience, and the things they already know. *Local knowledge,* then, is a term that helps us understand the diverse experiences of students and the particular aspects of their lives.

Rather than ignoring this local knowledge, teachers can rely on it as a foundation of learning. Anne Tewksbury-Frye (see "Teacher Portrait #7") reflects on the role of inquiry:

> Inquiry has its place with local [learning] because they have a lot of questions and I don't usually give them the answers. So they'll go out and investigate them and make connections for themselves . . . I think that is where a lot of great learning is born.

This awareness helps teachers design curriculum with questions that resonate with a student's experience. This is most critical for young people whose school experience continually underlines differences or perceived "deficits." According to Nieto (1999), ". . . [T]eachers need to build on what the children *do have,* rather than lament about what they *do not have*" (p. 7). When the content is more aligned with the truth of students' lives, they gain tools that help them gain a voice in their community. Jean Berthiaume (see "Teacher Portrait #5"), who teaches in a rural high school, makes the point that he could talk about discrimination in the context of some faraway place but "why not begin with what they experience in the halls of their own high school?"

Basing curriculum decisions on students' experience means paying close attention to how they learn. One teacher comments: "This is what teaching is all about, when I get to step back and see what the student is going to make of it." Framing curriculum around students' questions reflects a pedagogical commitment to what is happening—and what might happen—in their minds.

> "We have come to realize that meaning matters and is not something that can be imparted from teacher to student. In a sense, all teachers can do is to 'make noise in their environment.' . . . [W]e have . . . no main line into the brains of our students. We are shapers of the environment . . . But in the end, what children make of what we provide is a function of what they construe from what we offer. Meanings are not given, they are made."
>
> Elliot Eisner (1999, p. 658)

"When they control the learning, they remember everything they do on their own."

In constructivist classrooms (Brooks & Brooks, 1993), questions are recognized as an important window into students' thinking and become the opening for further learning. Learning resembles problem solving, the complex cognitive work needed to resolve personal experience with something learned in school or a solution to an actual happening in the community. Learning happens from a rich mix of experiences; it is a multidimensional phenomenon. With local investigations, there is more of an authentic mix of experience, personal meaning, and nearby happenings—that mimics how students learn naturally.

A Progressive View of Place and Student Experience

"A primary responsibility of educators [is to] recognize in the concrete what surroundings are conducive to having experiences that lead to growth. Above all, they should know how to utilize the surroundings, physical and social, that exist so as to extract from them all that they have to contribute to building up of experiences that are worthwhile."

John Dewey (1938, p. 40)

Attending to a student's past, present, and future experience is fundamental to progressive education. The writings of John Dewey, the most notable voice of progressive education, give teachers insight into how school might be more engaging. Dewey suggests that rather than presenting material as a distant body of knowledge, teachers should use what is "already seen and felt and loved" (Dewey, 1902, p. 353) and translate the subject into "life-terms" (p. 352).

In the previous introductory quote, Dewey poses the ability to use the "surroundings" as a critical consideration of curriculum design. It is up to the teacher to determine what experiences in the local community are worthwhile. In Dewey's (1922) view, the skilled teacher does this with "ends-in-view" (p. 71). This is the nugget of Dewey's work clearly reflected in Wiggins and McTighe's work *Understanding by Design* (1998, 2005), which asks teachers to identify worthwhile experiences that build enduring understanding. Dewey (1938) believed it was the job of the teacher "to select the kind of present experiences that live fruitfully and creatively in subsequent experiences" (p. 28). In the progressive view, the intentionality of this process is the creative and intellectual realm of the teacher. In the image titled "The Gully Is a Favorite Textbook" from Dewey and Dewey's book *Schools of Tomorrow* (1915), a teacher in Alabama has suggested students learn to "read" a local gully.

John Dewey posed that both knowledge of the subject *and an understanding of the student* are part of the art of teaching. In order for the student to have worthwhile learning experiences, the teacher presents—or the student encounters—an obstacle that creates a need to learn. This "craving . . . supplies motive for the learning. An end—*which is the child's own* [emphasis added]—carries him on to possess the means of its accomplishment" (Dewey, 1902, pp. 353–354). As noted earlier, having a vision of where an experience might take the learner involves teachers developing the skill to orchestrate the connections. Such mental investment or ownership of the learning process is key to conducting local investigations.

Lastly, Dewey posed that the social relations of a child and his or her developing sense of agency in a democracy is the primary purpose of school. Dewey's commitment to the practice of democracy in a social context underlines youth as a formative time to engage in democratic action. He maintained that "the child is an organic whole, intellectually, socially, and morally, as well as physically" (Dewey, 1909, pp. 8–9). The progressive view maintains that all of a learner's talent, intellect, and interests need to be given voice in order for school to be worthwhile for the student and for society.

The Critical Edge of Local Investigations

"Why not, for example, take advantage of the student's experience of life in those parts of the city neglected by the authorities to discuss the problems of pollution in the rivers and the question of poverty and the risks to health from the rubbish heaps in such areas? Why are there no rubbish heaps in the heart of the rich areas of the city? This question is considered 'in bad taste.' Pure demagogy. Almost subversive, say the defenders of democracy.

Why not discuss with students the concrete reality of their lives and that aggressive reality in which violence is permanent and where people are much more familiar with death than with life? Why not establish an 'intimate' connection between knowledge considered basic to any school curriculum and knowledge that is the fruit of the lived experience of these students as individuals?"

Paulo Friere (1998a, p. 36)

A critical view of one's place is rooted in the work of Paulo Friere who posed that students—of any age—should be taught to "read the world" in order to see the inequities and opportunity around them. Friere, the inspiration behind critical pedagogy, led a national literacy campaign for which he was jailed and exiled in his native Brazil in the 1960s. When he "taught the peasants to read, he also taught them to understand the reasons for their oppressed condition" (Wink, 2005, p. 90). In Friere's work, we come to understand the power of the term "place as text," as a perspective on literacy that extends the idea of a "sense of place" to taking responsible action.

Evoking Friere's view of literacy, David Gruenewald (2003a) invites educators to engage critically with their surroundings and suggests that the "texts" students and teachers should learn to "decode . . . are the images of their own concrete, situated experiences with the world" (p. 5). In order for students to "re-inhabit" their spaces, as Gruenewald suggests, not as a detached resident but as an educated, active learner, the agenda for schools shifts.

Giroux (1992) states, "Students must be offered the opportunities to read texts that both affirm and interrogate the complexities of their own histories . . . " (pp. 30–31). Students' lives need to be reflected in the choices, topics, and discourse of school. Ignoring these realities has grave implications for a student's sense of a personal future. When we examine our places, it must be with our eyes wide open as Friere suggests in the introductory quote.

By posing a more inclusive view toward sources of knowledge and student experience, critical theory offers a provocative lens to view the purpose of education. To answer their questions, students might investigate fair housing. E-waste, worker's wages, or the environmental impact of different forms of transportation might fuel an investigation. Their questions might lead to an authentic partnership with a community activist to solve a problem. Critical investigations continue to push out the "edge" of local inquiry and challenge long-held assumptions about what should be studied in school.

A teacher's ability to facilitate investigations into uncharted territory runs counter to common practice. At a time when teachers have less control over the time they spend with students, critical theory offers a way to "talk back." As Gruenewald (2003b) suggests, " . . . [the] claims of the primacy of place are revolutionary" (p. 627). Such a stance suggests organizing curriculum around the creative capabilities of teachers, students, *and the community* and asking questions that emerge from this cooperative undertaking.

Global Understanding Built from Local Learning

> "Local places provide the specific contexts from which reliable knowledge of global relationships emerge."
>
> *David Greenwood (2013, p. 94)*

Those who seek to *engage the local* maintain that understanding one's place can lead us to better understand all places. John Elder points out that knowing a place well should not exclude the ability to understand others. Educators "should cultivate a perspective of attentiveness to place—wherever one is—that lets one be in a new place too, with a strong sense of appreciation and responsibility for it" (Elder, 1999, p. 28). Educators in the Alaskan Native Knowledge Network support the "efficacy of an educational system that is grounded in the deep knowledge associated with a particular place, upon which a broader knowledge of the world can be built" (Barnhardt, 2008, p. 132).

Local places make up the whole of the world. An attention to place must coexist alongside the many ways young people come to understand that we inhabit a huge, wondrous, deeply troubled, spinning globe. Student understandings of the whole can be built from intimate learning experiences nearby. The significance of local learning underlines the ways that:

- Global understandings are best understood in local places.
- Local acts of kindness and generosity happen person-to-person.
- Work and careers are carried out in specific places.

- Learning things well is enhanced by an intimate connection to the thing under study.
- Students with global concerns need a lifeline to the local community in order to perform acts of service.

Teachers who consider themselves global studies educators can find ways to insert more local reference points in global learning. They can use a close lens alongside a more global view to better enrich learning. I learned this in a curriculum workshop with some foreign language teachers. Two French teachers who wanted to use food to teach grammar, vocabulary, and customs thought of ways students could experience "slow food" locally. A Latin teacher who wanted to teach about ancient Rome decided to ask her students, "What is a city?" and take a field trip to collect comparative data. She planned to compare gathering places, transportation, customs, housing, and the economy. All global studies teachers can add a "here-there" refrain to help students understand faraway places and global issues.

Such considerations do not replace the many wondrous opportunities for communication, collaboration, and personal growth generated from global interactions. Humanitarian gestures can travel electronically, and young people can grasp global issues online that can be creatively reinforced through global exchange. By grappling with a real-world issue "on the ground," students gain a perspective on what it might mean to become a global citizen. Focus on the local should never lessen opportunities for global understandings.

Doing Democracy

> "Involvement in community offers young people a chance to test themselves in new roles . . . to discover a place for themselves in the world, thereby creating for themselves a vision of a personal future."
>
> *Alice L. Halsted (quoted in Claus & Ogden, 1999, pp. 96–97)*

Smith and Sobel (2010) merge the terms *place-* and *community-based* to underline the highly civic nature of this learning as students build authentic partnerships with community members. In their phrasing, place- and community-based education is characterized by:

- a focus on local knowledge, issues, and phenomena and is potentially relevant to all subject areas,
- involvement from a wider range of adults who can serve as instructors and mentors,
- a starting point for lifelong understandings for all learners (youth and adults), and
- projects that require students to apply their knowledge, skills, and energy to community issues or problems (pp. 24–25).

Kids Consortium in Maine (www.kidsconsortium.org) maintains that meaningful service learning includes academic integrity, apprentice citizenship, and student ownership. By deepening the rigor and authenticity of the experience and putting kids at the center of the design and outcome, they reflect a growing view that service can be more than a single instance of serving food in a homeless shelter or holding a canned food drive. Good deeds done in isolation without any critical analysis often act as a "Band-Aid" and never really impact the cause of the problems. As one educator said, *"it is one thing to have kids clean up the river, but more importantly, they should 'go upriver' to see where the source of the problem is."* When students work with members of their community on real issues, the solutions they generate have the potential to effect real and lasting change.

Brian Williams. Used with permission.

Proponents of democratic schools claim that schools cannot effectively coach students in democracy if they are not democratic places themselves. Students learn from the total school experience, not just what happens, or is supposed to happen, in class. The competitive spirit that defines many classrooms prohibits true collaboration among students, and students and teachers, as well as the larger community. Citing the work of Purpel and Giroux, Wade (1997) writes, "Many of the structures of traditional schools involve seatwork, competitive grading, discouragement of collaboration, training in docility . . ." (p. 5). The way schools are structured, the way teachers and students treat each other, the topics they study, the food they eat, the rules they are asked to follow all form a "hidden curriculum" that affects what students actually learn in school and how they come to see their future.

Bridges of Accountability to Our Collective Future

> "It must be acknowledged that educators who wish to move in this direction will face a number of challenges, many of which are deeply rooted in the practices, structures, and philosophical premises commonly encountered in American schools."
>
> *Greg Smith (2002, p. 593)*

Teachers approach the task of curriculum design fortified with a mix of goals related to a student's experience, ways of knowing, sense of place, and personal agency. The curricular strategies in this book are based on using essential questions as a basis for curriculum design as put forth by Grant Wiggins and Jay McTighe (1998, 2005). Their work offers teachers a way to create curriculum and plan learning around questions. Using an approach called "backwards design," teachers identify the enduring understanding or big idea they want students to have grasped at the unit's end. They then take the required content and align the enduring understanding to how and what they want to teach. Teachers plan the learning activities in relation to this lasting understanding. In its very structure, it gives teachers ways to weave the larger purposes into the planned learning. It is not "just an activity" but a carefully crafted aspect of gaining new understanding. Essential questions based on standards, such as *"What is the difference between weather and climate?"* or *"What is public art?"* or *"What does equal mean?"* (a question related to math and social studies!), all can be pursued meaningfully in local places.

Standards and Standardization

In general, the world of standards, and the heavy burden that it places on teachers, runs counter to the view of their creative capacity as artists. However, standards when used appropriately are not antithetical to excellent teaching and deep learning: "Standards, originally designed to organize and promote a coherent curriculum are not being used as originally intended. . . . first praised, then appropriated, and most recently used as a sledge hammer by federal and state policy makers. . . ." (Darling-Hammond & Sykes, 1999, p. 345).

Despite the intensity of the current climate of high-stakes testing, teachers find ways to design assessments that are meaningful and useful. They find it is not a mixed message to say "raise test scores" and "increase achievement" and "learn outside the classroom" if assessment goals are clearly defined. In the process, they find ways to not get lost in the diminished expectations that current calls for accountability represent. A larger purpose can house the mastery of the skills and knowledge of specific subjects—as well as bigger, more important questions. Standards can provide the basis for a whole-school and district-wide reorientation to the local environment (Lieberman, 2013).

Structuring investigations in local places is challenging in the current climate but aligns with many initiatives such as the Common Core (www.corestandards.

org), which offers (Anchor Standard W.CCR.7) a fundamental literacy skill as the ability to "conduct short as well as more sustained research projects based on focus questions, demonstrating understanding of the subject under investigation."

The authors of the new *Framework for K-12 Science Education: Practices, Crosscutting Concepts, and Core Ideas* (National Research Council, 2012) suggest that "the learning experiences provided for students should engage them with fundamental questions about the world and with how scientists have investigated and found answers to these questions" (p. 9).

The social scientists who wrote the new *College, Career, and Civic Life (C3) Framework for Social Studies State Standards* encourage the use of compelling and supporting questions, both teacher- and student-generated, as a central element of the teaching and learning process and maintain that this, ". . . along with the curricular content and the distinctive habits of mind from the other social science disciplines, informs students' investigations and contributes to an inquiry process for social studies" (NCSS, 2013, p. 17).

Authentic investigations can foster higher-order thinking, authentic problem solving, and a cognitive richness that promotes academic achievement. Wiggins and McTighe (2013) maintain that "there is no conflict . . . in advocating a question-based curricular framework in an accountability system that looks for specific knowledge, skill, and understanding of content . . . only students who have learned for understanding can perform well on rigorous testing" (pp. 26–27). Teachers find ways for student work to address the standards as well as reflect larger goals inherent in local investigations (see Figure 1.1).

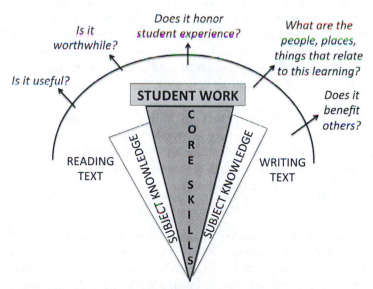

FIGURE 1.1 Standards-based Context of Local Learning

Our Curriculum Matters. Used with permission.

This ability to embed knowledge and skills within a more meaningful context aligns with the following beliefs about teaching in the 21st century:

- Framing content as questions engages the learner and offers a model for building knowledge and skills as well as a way to build understanding of the "big ideas" of the disciplines.
- Using this approach as a frame, the work that students do can be relevant and rigorous.
- Social sciences and the arts—recess and healthy lunches!—are as important for learners as math, science, and technology.
- The appropriate use of technology is as a resource for learning, not as an end in itself.
- We need an educational system with an intelligent balance of some testing alongside rich, engaging curriculum and multiple forms of assessment.

★★★★★★★★★★

When people work together and solve problems they generate a new vision of schools and community. As the questions get bigger and the work more worthwhile, teachers and students reframe tasks and claim more space in the curriculum. Engaged local learning gives students opportunities to learn history better, understand poetry, conduct scientific inquiry, and express themselves through artistic mediums, personal expression, and civic engagement and, in the process, brings schools into a community's active participation in democracy.

When students pursue authentic questions, it is not "just an assignment" but has the potential to generate a new vision of one's self and one's sense of social engagement. It is not just "learning" about a problem. It takes the understanding to a deeper level of knowing to the point of action. The experience, one way or another, will leave the student with a sense of what he might be capable of. In this way, teachers are faced with the inner dimensions of this work. As Paulo Friere (2004) considered:

> . . . To the extent that we become capable of transforming our world, of naming our own surroundings, of apprehending, of making sense of things, of deciding, of choosing, of valuing, and, finally, of ethicizing the world, our mobility within it and through history necessarily comes to involve dreams toward whose realization we struggle.
>
> *(p. 7)*

We do not, as educators, get to prescribe dreams. We can hope, we can plan, we can give students rich provocative experiences that rattle their sense of complacency, but we do not get to define what will happen or what path a student takes. Yet, as Friere suggests, we are entwined with our students' individual dreams *at all times.* Experiences in community offer students opportunities to learn in different ways and get feedback from different people. A student's moral compass can be set by a combination of rich and challenging interactions with people and places. It does, indeed, take a village to raise a child.

****

References

Barnhardt, R. (2008). Creating a place for indigenous knowledge in education: The Alaska Native Knowledge Network. In D. Gruenewald & G. Smith (Eds.), *Place-based education in the global age: Local diversity* (pp. 113–133). Hillsdale, NJ: Lawrence Erlbaum Associates, Taylor and Francis Group.

Brooks, J., & Brooks, M. (1993). *In search of understanding: The case for constructivist classrooms.* Alexandria, VA: Association for Supervision and Curriculum Development.

Chawla, L. (1998). Significant life experiences revisited: A review of research on sources of environmental sensitivity. *Journal of Environmental Education, 29*(3), 11–21. http://dx.doi.org/10.1080/00958969809599114

Claus, J., & Ogden, C. (Eds.). (1999). *Service learning for youth empowerment and social change.* New York, NY: Peter Lang.

Darling-Hammond, L., & Sykes, G. (Eds.). (1999). *Teaching as the learning profession: Handbook of policy and practice.* San Francisco, CA: Jossey-Bass.

Delpit, L. (2012). *"Multiplication is for white people": Raising expectations for other people's children.* New York, NY: The New Press.

Dewey, J. (1902). The child and the curriculum. In R. D. Archambault (Ed.), *John Dewey on education: Selected writings* (pp. 339–358). Chicago, IL: University of Chicago Press.

Dewey, J. (1909). *Moral principles in education.* Boston, MA: Houghton-Mifflin.

Dewey, J. (1922). The nature of aims. In R. D. Archambault (Ed.), *John Dewey on education: Selected writings* (pp. 70–80). Chicago, IL: University of Chicago Press.

Dewey, J. (1938). *Experience and education.* New York, NY: Macmillan.

Dewey, J., & Dewey, E. (1915). *Schools of tomorrow.* New York, NY: E. P. Dutton.

Doll, W. (1993). *A post-modern perspective on curriculum.* New York, NY: Teachers College Press.

Eisner, E. W. (1999). The uses and limits of performance assessment. *Phi Delta Kappan, 80*(9), 658–660.

Elder, J. (1999). In pursuit of a bioregional curriculum: An interview with John Elder. *Orion Afield: Working for Nature and Community, 3*(2), 26–28.

Feld, S., & Basso, K. (1996a). Introduction. In S. Feld & K. Basso (Eds.), *Senses of place* (p. 5). Sante Fe, NM: School of American Research Press.

Feld, S., & Basso, K. (Eds.) (1996b). *Senses of place.* Sante Fe, NM: School of American Research Press.

Friere, P. (1998a). *Pedagogy of freedom: Ethics, democracy, and civic courage.* Lanham, MD: Rowman and Littlefield.

Friere, P. (1998b). *Teachers as cultural workers: Letters to those who dare to teach.* Boulder, CO: Westview Press.

Friere, P. (2004). *Pedagogy of indignation.* Boulder, CO: Paradigm.

Giroux, H. (1992). *Border crossings: Cultural workers and the politics of education.* New York, NY: Routledge.

Giroux, H. (2013). *America's education deficit and the war on youth.* New York, NY: Monthly Review Press.

Greenwood, D. (2013). A critical theory of place-conscious education. In R. B. Stevenson, M. Brody, J. Dillon, & A. E. J. Wals (Eds.), *International handbook on environmental education* (pp. 93–100). New York, NY: Routledge.

Gruenewald, D. (2003a). The best of both worlds: A critical pedagogy of place. *Educational Researcher, 32*(4), 3–12. http://dx.doi.org/10.3102/0013189X032004003

Gruenewald, D. (2003b). Foundations of place: A multidisciplinary framework for place-conscious education. *American Educational Research Journal, 40*(3), 619–654. http://dx.doi.org/10.3102/00028312040003619

Haas, T., & Nachtigal, P. (1998). *Place value: An educator's guide to good literature on rural lifeways, environments and purposes of education.* Charleston, WV: ERIC Clearinghouse on Rural Education and Small Schools No. RC021543. (ERIC Document Reproduction Service No. ED420461)

Henderson, J. G., & Kesson, K. R. (2004). *Curriculum wisdom: Educational decisions in democratic societies.* Upper Saddle River, NJ: Pearson.

Horton, M. (1990). *The long haul.* New York, NY: Doubleday.

Kozol, J. (2005). *The shame of the nation: The restoration of apartheid schooling in America.* New York, NY: Three Rivers Press.

Lieberman, G. L. (2013). *Education and the environment: Creating standards-based programs in schools and districts.* Cambridge, MA: Harvard Education Press.

National Council for the Social Studies (NCSS). (2013). *The college, career, and civic life (C3) framework for social studies state standards: Guidance for enhancing the rigor of K-12 civics, economics, geography, and history.* Silver Spring, MD: NCSS.

National Research Council. (2012). *A framework for K-12 science education: Practices, crosscutting concepts, and core ideas.* Committee on a Conceptual Framework for New K-12 Science Education Standards. Board on Science Education, Division of Behavioral and Social Sciences and Education. Washington, DC: The National Academies Press.

Nieto, S. (1999). *The light in their eyes: Creating multicultural learning communities.* New York, NY: Teachers College Press.

Orr, D. W. (1992). *Ecological literacy: Education and the transition to a postmodern world.* Albany: State University of New York Press.

Perrone, V. (1998). *Teacher with a heart: Reflections on Leonard Covello and community.* New York, NY: Teachers College Press.

Smith, G. (2002). Place-based education: Learning to be where we are. *Phi Delta Kappan, 83*(8), 584–594.

Smith, G., & Sobel, D. (2010). *Place- and community-based education in schools.* New York, NY: Routledge.

Tyack, D., & Tobin, W. (1994). The "grammar" of schooling: Why has it been so hard to change? *American Educational Research Journal, 31*(3), 453–479. http://dx.doi.org/10.3102/00028312031003453

Wade, R. C. (Ed.). (1997). *Community service learning: A guide to including service in the public school curriculum.* Albany: State University of New York Press.

Wells, G. (Ed.). (2001). *Action, talk and text: Learning and teaching through inquiry.* New York, NY: Teachers College Press.

Wiggins, G., & McTighe, J. (1998). *Understanding by design* (1st ed.). Alexandria, VA: Association for Supervision and Curriculum Development.

Wiggins, G., & McTighe, J. (2005). *Understanding by design* (2nd ed.). Alexandria, VA: Association for Supervision and Curriculum Development.

Wiggins, G., & McTighe J. (2013). *Essential questions: Opening doors to student understanding.* Alexandria, VA: Association for Supervision and Curriculum Development.

Wink, J. (2005). *Critical pedagogy: Notes from the field* (3rd ed.). Upper Saddle River, NJ: Pearson.

2

HOW DOES PLACE-BASED EDUCATION WORK IN REAL CLASSROOMS?

When questions are asked and explored in the places where we live, the synergy that develops positions the teacher and the learner in a new relationship with each other, the community, and the answers that emerge. Learning *how* to manage these interactions in the land of high-stakes testing and stringent accountability is a creative journey for the teacher. Gay Craig (see "Teacher Portrait #3") describes place-based education this way:

> . . . it's local, and it's connected to students in a way that they can identify with. It's either a problem in their community or an event that's happening, or it could be a geological [phenomenon]. But [it's something] they're all familiar with . . . so it means something to them. And then we ask questions about it.

The work entailed in local investigations is a more dynamic and energetic undertaking than gathering around a static exchange of information seated in a classroom. As teachers work to integrate this kind of learning, they quickly find that big questions take up more room and more energy. They need to create structures that accommodate this more personal and authentic connection. As the work continues, the teacher's view of what can happen in school continues to shift, expand, and grow. This chapter is about the challenges of structuring learning around investigations and how teachers manage the implementation of an inquiry-based pedagogy amidst the many demands of the workplace.

Curriculum Example: Making a Map

Examining the size, intent, and implications of a question helps us understand the ways inquiry can change the scope of teaching and assessment and require a more complex design analysis. This chapter begins with a look at how a traditional mapping project changes as a teacher considers the different elements of the design process. It also introduces the reader to the curricular terms and considerations used throughout the book. The National Geography Standards (Geography Education Standards Project, 1994) are used in this section to underline the role of standards in developing questions.

Consider the question, *"Where are we?"*

National Geography Standard #1: The geographically informed person knows and understands: how to use maps and other geographical representations, tools, and technologies to acquire, process, and report information from a spatial perspective.

A traditional student response or "answer" to this question would be a map with specific features required by the teacher. There would likely be a lesson on geographical features that presents a model of a completed map with the required elements such as landmarks, routes, and physical features. Given new technologies, a modern-day map might look a little snazzier than the maps created by our grandparents, but a standards-based response to *where we are* in geospatial terms would illustrate a student's geography skills. The teacher would assign and assess the use of these skills as well as other traits such as artistic design, neatness, accuracy, or completeness.

Different themes could make the maps serve a specific purpose or be more engaging for the student:

- If the teacher wanted to make the mapmaking more personal, she could ask her students to think about their special places. She might share other writers' views toward "special places" from books, poetry, or local residents and suggest they think about "a place I love to play," "safe places to skateboard," or "best places to eat/hang out." Students would have choices in terms of what was actually on the map, but still be required to use their geography skills.

National Geography Standard #6: The geographically informed person knows and understands: how culture and experience influence people's perceptions of places and regions.

- If the question, "Where are we?" were approached from an interdisciplinary view, students might integrate different content into the maps. They still might use a variety of geography skills and tools but demonstrate their understanding of other subjects—in relation to the place they were studying. Students could interpret historic sites, geologic markers, ecological events, and animal habitat to express particular aspects of a place.

Katie Wyndorf. Used with permission.

- From another perspective, a teacher who wants students to understand changes in the community might ask them to examine demographic indicators and develop their own interpretive tools to represent data on the map. Thinking of maps in a more complex way, students might research what they see locally alongside similar changes in other places. The research could involve an ongoing digital dialogue between students about the nature of community, equity, and progress.
- In a more global approach, the question of *"Where are we?"* might be employed to explore world cultures and better understand ourselves and others in a global context. *How does where we live compare to where others live? How does this impact how we live? Do other places deal with flooding, draught, urban sprawl in the same way we do?* Students could map protected places, threatened spaces, and stories of human resilience. Google Maps (www.google.com/maps) could be created that are highly interactive and share students' insights and questions.

National Geography Standard #10: The geographically informed person knows and understands: the characteristics, distribution, and complexity of Earth's cultural mosaics.

- If the teacher wanted the map to serve a specific audience, students might make a map to introduce new Americans to their new home and help them find their own answer to *"Where are we?"* Students might include the best route to school, public transportation, and other points of interest and interview newcomers about how their new home compares to where they came from. They might have to navigate language barriers, research other places in the world, and explore values different than their own. Their final maps might be produced in different languages and shared with others in a way that best served the people that were going to use it.

• If a teacher wanted to be more attentive to specific Common Core Standards (www.corestandards.org) she might ask students to create well-written and well-researched descriptions of the places on their map that were "informative [and] explanatory" and "convey[ed] complex ideas and information clearly and accurately" (Anchor Standard W.CCR.2). She might ask students to use a variety of sources in order to "integrate and evaluate information presented in diverse media and formats, including visually, quantitatively, and orally" (Anchor Standard SL.CCR.2).

Other Design Considerations

Teachers wrestle with how to word essential questions to fit their purposes. One teacher considered amending the question to *"Where are we now?"* The *now* indicated that her 12-year-old students may have been many other places before ending up in this place and in their lifetime had yet to experience other places. It introduced the possibility of seeing this place as one place among many places, thereby helping students see that understanding where we live is a transferable, lifelong skill.

In a more critical lens, we might think of the question as a reference to where we are as a society. Have we made progress or regressed? James Boggs and Grace Lee Boggs (1974), activists in Detroit, Michigan, asked: *"What time is it on the clock of the world?"* (p. 168). Where are we in the long view of history? Such a question invites students to think about the quality of their lives in relationship to others both in time and place.

Or a teacher might use the question, "Where are we in our ability to care for each other?" to engage her students in investigating safety and health issues in the community by evaluating social service agencies. The teacher might ask students to explore the neighborhood to map out different needs and services, conduct interviews at different sites, and pursue the questions raised in the interviews. As the unit unfolds, the teacher needs to track more complex design considerations:

• *What goes on the map?* In a community service project in which the class selects an agency and sponsors a workday in that organization, students might "map" the work they did in terms of the people they had contact with. They might tackle the issue of how people in the neighborhood get access to services. To unravel this problem, they may need to collaborate with the city planner, different agencies, and community organizers. They might decide to include the narratives of different people gathered from the interviews. They might decide that a worthwhile culminating activity is a "map" that rates how accessible the agencies in their community are, using criteria for equity and efficiency that they determine with their community partners.

- *Who is this map for?* The students might decide to show their work to the city council where they raise questions about the government's responsibility toward individuals. The mapping task takes on a larger purpose; the result of their work is used by the community. The teacher may have envisioned part of that outcome, but not as it ended up. The students and the community have become "partners" in curriculum design.

City High School. Used with permission.

- *How is the work assessed?* The teacher is challenged to chart these larger intentions. She might want students to learn basic geography skills, public speaking, computation of data, and how to clearly present information, collaborate, and plan. She also may want students to learn about justice and equity, gain empathy and understanding about where they live, and develop skills to act on these complexities. The content, process, and outcomes are tracked as the work moves forward.
- *What do the students accomplish?* A multitude of skills emerge from this real work. Through different mediums—dialogue, artwork, documentaries, video—students can express their new learning. In designing a final assessment task, the teacher will plan how to record evidence of new knowledge and skills that might not be the same for every student.

An assessment tool that addresses all the aspects of this larger work might be a document that teachers and students create together. It can be part of a transparent process, amended and used as an ongoing, formative assessment as well as a final reflection. Criteria such as those listed in the Assessment Criteria of Final Project box (below) could be used to design a more detailed rubric with performance descriptions that provide what "meeting the standard," and so forth, looks like in a specific assignment.

ASSESSMENT CRITERIA OF FINAL PROJECT

___Geography skills: What skills did you use to create this project?

___Literacy (or other) skills: What communication skills did you use to create this project?

___Interpretation of place: What new understanding did you gain about your community?

___Collaboration: What did you learn from working with other people? What were the challenges and what were the rewards?

___Taking action: What contribution did you personally make to this project? What impact do you feel the work of the whole group had?

___Reflection: What did this mean to you? Are there any ways that you might imagine using your new skills or insight in the future?

The purpose of the mapping activity has grown. The lesson still contains recognizable pieces of a traditional geography lesson but with a larger capacity. The work has expanded in relation to the question asked and the places that are explored. New, unanticipated learning and skills emerge from this larger work. A teacher has learned to merge the *"know-how"* with the *"what-if?"*

The student's capacities have grown as well. If the mapping activity is worthwhile, the student has gained new skills—specific mapping skills, perhaps interview skills and computer skills—as well as insight into one's role in the community. He might be able to transfer the skill of understanding his own place to understanding others. Redefining the actual purpose and process of student work helps us better communicate our purposes in regard to a student's experience, mastery of subject, and relationship with his community.

Making Space for Larger Learning

In order for a question to foster new understanding, it must be claimed—both cognitively and emotionally—by the student. Direct experience grappling with a local question—or a global question made local—has a better chance of gaining traction in the mind of the learner. If the question is only clear in the teacher's mind, if it stays inert on the page or is quieted by protocol, there is no way for the student to own it. Or as Dewey (1902) puts it, the teacher has failed to "psychologize" the material, to "turn over and translate [the material] into the . . . immediate experience" (p. 351). The challenge for the teacher is to generate the questioning activity in the mind of a learner and transfer ownership of the question to the learner—to "hand it over."

This process of "handing it over" can happen when the student engages with nearby people and places and has the opportunity to act, express, interact, name, and re-name that world. Teachers make space for these new kinds of interactions. This is how it first happened to me:

> I was on a bird walk with 23 fifth-graders when we happened on to a pond in springtime. We had been trying to keep quiet but being outdoors on a beautiful spring day already had posed its own challenges. When the students saw the pond, all bets were off. Within seconds we were in the midst of high-level scientific inquiry. Students' questions about eggs, salamanders, and water temperature swirled in a frenzy of high energy and high interest that was totally unanticipated. I would have been crazy to stick to the topic of birds when all 23 minds were focused on the wonder of a pond in springtime. I needed to let go of my plans and step back and let the pond energy happen. I had to provide safety and some direction—and find ways to help them answer their many questions—but the learning was happening between them and the pond. I gained a profound lesson about teaching that continues to spiral though my career as I learn and relearn to step back and let students engage in the learning on their own terms . . . and that the more I make space for that, the better it gets.

Such unexpected moments of authentic engagement may be more likely outside of the classroom, but they can be intentionally created anywhere. It involves the intricate, creative process of putting "obstacles" in the cognitive path of students that become the context for new understanding. Edward Chittenden (2005) makes this observation while watching four-year-olds observe millipedes:

> It strikes me that the millipedes ha[d] taken the foreground as teachers. The classroom teacher artfully stepped aside so that the animals, in their myriapodal ways, could give the children firsthand lessons in fundamentals of the natural world. . . . You may want [the millipede] to run, jump, or hop, or eat something else, but it stays with its own rules. . . .
>
> *(p. 163)*

As Chittenden suggests, the teacher skillfully orchestrates the opportunity and then artfully steps aside. The teacher brings in the millipede, but the millipede does the teaching. Space is made for the students' experience; it is not all controlled by the teacher. It is not that the teacher steps back completely and lets whatever happen, happen. It's about effectively using the experience of meeting up face-to-face with a millipede (quilt, person, old house, document, or tide pool) and allowing students to make their own sense of that.

While a millipede might not seem an enduring metaphor for teachers seeking to explore history lessons, literature, or larger issues of social justice or equity, it reminds us that actual experiences must happen in order for thinking to change. This is the same dynamic when a teacher takes on a question about race, sexual identity, or poverty. Any authentic question will require more time to pursue. In the case of the millipede, the teacher carves out time and space for students to wonder about, understand, and articulate—on their own terms—what a millipede is all about. In the process, she teaches the skills of asking and answering questions; weaves in concepts and skills related to understanding a millipede, such as life cycles or drawing the body parts; and responds to challenges set forth by the questions. They may talk about how the millipede travels, draw it, write stories about it, and enhance its image digitally, but these activities are generated from the initial experience with the millipede.

Teachers find when students engage with the real world, the "figuring out" is more complex; the student may take a path not readily apparent to the teacher. This complex work involves tasks my colleague Charlie Rathbone (personal communication, September 2008) defines as the essence of learning: "*It is the activity of the brain asking questions about a 'difficulty' and getting to a new place that is the learning . . . it's all about forming new connections, re-learning, and resolving complications of old thoughts. Nothing happens until the student gets the question.*"

Many teachers agree in theory that school should be more "real" but find it challenging to bring something "alive" into the classroom. The teacher has to create new structures to handle these more complex interactions. The work changes; tasks are moved around, reordered, and constructed differently. As the teacher sees how her students respond, she might come to view their capabilities in a new light. "You do something that works, then add it to your repertoire, and then you try something else," one teacher comments. It is an iterative process, and each moment of learning informs another.

> *"We're following their questions, and they're making connections in the community, and they need to know things that they don't already know. We don't always know what that is."*

While our visit to the pond was serendipitous, a teacher might intentionally plan a wide range of experiences based on authentic discovery. It could be a highly challenging intellectual discussion that takes place as students sit in a park or a messy, muddy endeavor when students are in a river collecting data or cleaning out garbage. Questions are generated from the experience. The cognitive task of working out the question needs to be real enough to endure in the learner's thinking. When the student learns from a problem he has worked through, he is then is able to organize, for his own purposes, a multitude of skills, information, and processes that are more permanent. It is the authenticity of the investigation that causes the disruption.

The Inquiry Process

Teachers use questions for different purposes. The complexity and context vary according to grade, subject, students, and community. Teachers need to spend time arriving at a question that will drive the investigation as well as serve the student and the purpose of the lesson. The points of intersection lie within the student, the subject, the place, and future uncharted possibilities. Students in one class might raise questions about examining stereotypes in their community. Questions in another class may be more confined to concrete circumstances, such as changes in temperature or soil erosion, depending on what parameters the teacher has set. All kinds of questions are possible, and it is up to the teacher how she will contain, control, use, and follow them.

> *"There is that inquiry spirit going on."*

In a classroom built on inquiry, the collective asking and answering of questions becomes the work of a school day. Routine tasks and skills are housed in this larger frame. When the teacher believes that learning is about figuring things out, her job becomes more of a problem-poser and question-asker than a "presenter of information." The archetypal lesson plan is created from the teacher's ability to pose a problem and give students time to work it out. Sometimes it takes a long time for the student to get to the question. Clearly identifying the steps of the process can help the student and the teacher.

Two school districts (Partnership for Change; http://partnershipvt.org) near where I live are in the process of exploring the promise of personalized learning.

In Winooski, Vermont, teachers created a space for students to follow their questions. It is called an "I-Lab," and the design of the space is geared toward the work that students do to learn about a topic in which they are interested. The plan sits on the wall:

THINK IT ** LEARN IT ** MAKE IT ** SHARE IT

When the stages of learning are developed and articulated to this degree, as they can be in any inquiry project, students can be more effectively involved in assessment. They may know what they want to learn but are struggling to figure out their question, or they may be moving too fast to the "MAKE IT" stage and need to stay longer in the "LEARN IT" phase. Breaking out the elements facilitates communication between teacher and student and invites self-reflection and a chance for the learner to be more invested in the question.

> *"Work is more complex because they have to resolve their own knowledge of something that they are familiar with—with something new."*

Ellen Temple (see "Teacher Portrait #4") suggests that authentic learning involves asking a question in a way that might not have been asked just that way before. The problem is new and so is the "answer." When making a community video, Kate observed that the tasks students are engaged in are "really new" and acknowledged that it is sometimes a "wild ride" to accommodate their completion. What guides her is the need to pay attention to the questions that need answering, not a need to get to the end of a prescribed text. They write the text—literally and figuratively—as they go. She realized that the students could use class time to call and arrange interviews and that "class might be [more like] a meeting than a class." Kate cited what a different feeling it was for teachers and students to start the class with the question, "What do we need to do today?" followed by a 10-minute dialogue that uncovers how some people might need to work on their questions, others need to use a phone, some might need the computer lab, and a few others are ready to leave the building and conduct their interview. "The other day," she reported, "after we got rolling and everyone was doing what they needed to do, there were only two people left in the classroom!"

A teacher might write in her lesson plan book something like this:

> Begin class by asking about final projects; where is everyone at? Use Kayla's plan (check with Kayla before school) as an example. Talk about the ways that she has connected with different people to interview and arranged times to meet with them. Ask Kayla to share a strategy that worked. Ask students

to pair-share and do similar brainstorming about strategies (15 minutes). Ask students to share with the class. Hand out schedule for rest of week, and ask students to write out their plan that details what they need to do.

An assignment of Jean's helps us see how the inquiry process directs the curriculum. He wanted his students to investigate the issue of free trade globally and how it impacted them locally. He began with some broad questions about free trade and asked students to brainstorm what they thought was important to consider. He had determined the focus, but his students had not yet identified their questions. Issues emerged such as environment, job security, high prices, quality of food, and impact on indigenous communities. He then prompted students to think about how these issues worked locally. They discussed questions such as the following: How does the price we pay affect growers in other parts of the world? What would it take for trade to be more equitable? How should consumers make these different decisions? Jean then asked students to brainstorm a list of local places where these different decisions were made. "One student wanted to go to the day care and find out how they decided what food to buy; I never would have thought of that," said Jean. His job, after students had identified the questions, was to support their foray into the community to find answers.

THE INQUIRY PROCESS

___Pose a problem (or question).
___Frame questions about problem (or question).
___Pose possible solutions/analyze, evaluate.
___Organize plan for finding solutions (might be structured as informal inquiry or long-term research project).
___Conduct investigations/research in community.
___Share findings with chosen audience.
___Identify implications/next steps and possible actions.

Where Do Questions Come From?

Questions come from students, subjects, and the communities in which we live (see Figure 2.1). They might emerge directly from the students' experience or from a new insight that an act of service poses. They will come from curriculum documents and directives. They can be utilized in different ways.

While the process of inquiry depends on the question being new in some way for the student, it does not mean that all questions are new. Investigations can focus on age-old questions. Inquiry can be used to examine some of the ideas that have sustained civilizations over time, such as *"What is justice?"* or *"What is a life well*

WHERE DO QUESTIONS COME FROM?
Some things you will teach because you have to.
Much of the content you are required to teach in schools appears because somebody, somewhere (often far away in place and time) decided that it needed to be taught. Oftentimes these assumptions are adopted by Districts and are reflected in curriculum documents. This dictated material may or may not act much like questions when a teacher first meets up with it, but she can often provide a context that makes sense to the student. Students always need a reason to learn. Questions help.
Questions come from the core disciplines and related standards.
Standards represent the big ideas about how the world functions. Wiggins and McTighe encourage us to take the standards and turn them into questions "that evoke possible answers" (1998, p. 27). For example, the science standard "interdependence" can become the question; "How are living things dependent on one another?" An art standard about the use of different mediums might be addressed through the question: "How can I best express myself?" Uncovering the questions within content provide students with something to grapple with. Questions are the entry points that provide pathways to the required learning.
Questions come from students.
Regardless of curriculum requirements, students generate questions about themselves, their world, and the things that they are learning. If the teacher is open to new discoveries and exploration, the questions will be given more room. Sometimes they emerge as questions; other times they are needs or interests that the teacher can bridge to the curriculum. To varying degrees, teachers can find ways to build curriculum around the questions that students have.
Questions will come from the community in which you teach.
If teachers open up their classroom to the realities outside their classroom—whether it be how seeds grow or how people treat each other—the questions will come. They will come from the needs and characteristics and particular histories and inhabitants of a place. They will emerge when students go exploring and interact with the people, places, and things in the community. They may not always be the questions teachers are planning for. Questions arise from the relationships that develop with people in the community when students are out working and exploring new ways of interacting and becoming.

FIGURE 2.1

Amy B. Demarest, Place-based Curriculum Design: Exceeding Standards through Local Investigations. © Routledge, 2015.

lived?" or "What is education for?" Students can be invited into an authentic exploration of some universal question, examine the wisdom of the "ancients," and make their own decisions about what would be a good answer for themselves.

"Curriculum works best when you present some teaching up front and then there's an organic . . . buy in from students."

The matter of who owns the question can be a moral stumbling block for some teachers. Teachers ask how they can plan for including student voice and authentic discovery when the student is not present in the planning process. There are different responses to this dilemma at different times. In general, the most important thing is how the learner views the question. A student can get very engaged in a question raised by someone else if a process for "handing it over" is in place. They also can be totally unengaged in questions the teacher might be convinced will enrapture each learner. Some teachers are more skilled at creating space for students to find their own questions. Ideally, it is a reciprocal process, where the teacher constantly seeks ways to transfer ownership to the student so the learning happens.

While the basic premise of inquiry is that a teacher needs to acknowledge all students' questions, some questions will serve the learner better than others. Students need coaching to identify a good question that will carry them through research and address their interests. Maintaining the student's sense of ownership during the process is critical. Facilitating inquiry is an art.

> ***"When the kids get to have control over it . . . it becomes what they want it to become."***

When students connect in these deeper ways, they find new ways to become a partner in directing the learning experience. This is what Kate referred to as the "green light." When students show her what works, it informs the decisions she makes as a teacher. Kate describes that there is a constant bartering necessary to coax them to engage in the work. "I'm competing for a space in their life and in their head," she says, "and I want to win." If a student says, "This is boring," Kate responds:

> That is information I need . . . not that it's all going to be a party, but you need to listen to students when they tell you how it makes them feel and work with that . . . and sometimes they just have to do [what I say] . . . but sometimes there is a negotiated place we get to.

Kate describes this need to shepherd the process: "You don't just look at the kids and say, 'What do you want to learn?' . . . That's crazy! You have to frame it and guide it and manage it." A teacher needs to be comfortable as a designer of experiences with "ends-in-view" (Dewey, 1922, p. 71). She has an idea about the result of the work; certain elements may be identified at the outset, but it is not completely defined. She is able to manage the challenges of making space for authentic questions and learning from a variety of sources.

Inquiry Takes Time

The process of inquiry—making space and time to ask and answer questions and process complex outcomes—is not easily contained in the traditional school day. "Schools are about DO, DO, DO!" Kate said. "You need to take time out to think." Teachers want their students to write, draw, and figure things out on their own but acknowledge that quiet thinking time is hard to schedule. "I am going to have my students keep their own journals this year," says one teacher. Another says, "After they are outside, I try to give them time to write about what they saw, but we hardly ever have the time."

> *"They learn a lot from each other if you ever give them time to do it, right? [It] takes time and you have to get out of the way."*

In defining the elements of a culture of inquiry, Wiggins and McTighe (2013) concur that students need the time to process new learning, build meaning, talk things out, and share ideas. They suggest that this time is different than direct instruction for skill acquisition or the time needed to practice or transfer these new skills (p. 84). Carving out the time and naming the specific need goes a long way to making it happen.

> *"There is a structure . . . but it's a little noisier."*

In authentic tasks, there is a higher level of collaboration and self-direction. This takes time. When students learn to work together to define and solve a problem, there is a shared interest in completing the task. Students are not working on disconnected parts but are seeking an integrated whole answer together. A student working on a video in Jean's class said, "We had to know each other's narrative and what it meant so it would all make sense." Collaboration was not an assignment; it was an essential ingredient of the outcome.

How Big Is the Question?

Teachers who use inquiry extensively believe that being able to think critically is an important part of the process. Jean uses the term "critical consumers" that he says: " . . . is like the Wizard of Oz. . . . learning how to pull back the curtain a little bit to show you the guts of how [the world] is working." Jean sees school as a way for students to find their way in the world and deal with the larger questions that face society: "If we are not dealing with the big questions, then what is the purpose?"

For many teachers, the ultimate goal is for students to practice democracy through civic engagement. A question such as "Does everyone here have enough to eat?" is "bigger" than a question about how to grow potatoes. Students may have good reasons to explore both. Often the "bigger" questions can lead to acts of service. Communicating the larger purpose within a curricular context is challenging. Jean observes:

> Service learning has to be organic; you can't just take a lesson and "boom" make it happen . . . there are too many variables . . . how to build ownership, how will you start . . . will you give students a "menu" to choose from, or will it emerge from an inquiry? There are so many different levels of teacher direction.

With civic engagement, as with all authentic inquiry, a teacher can't always predict the outcome. Jean notes that " . . . teaching students how to be democratic citizens or agents of change . . . I don't know all the ways." While you cannot plan for what will arise, you can create an openness, opportunity, and space for students to make choices.

"You can't just throw global warming at them and expect them to deal with it."

In considering how big the work will be, teachers need to take into account a student's emotional and intellectual readiness. An issue might be too difficult given that student's level of maturity. David Sobel (1996) in *Beyond Ecophobia* asks us to think about this when we explore sensitive issues with young people. He suggests *"no tragedies before fourth grade"* and warns that *"if we prematurely ask students to deal with problems beyond their control . . . [and] to solve the mammoth problems of an adult world, then . . . we cut them off from the possible sources of their own strength"* (p. 5). The learning *and the doing* have to be accessible to all students intellectually, emotionally, and morally.

A teacher at the school for Social Justice High School in Chicago (http:// sj.lvlhs.org) spoke about tackling the big problems and how he saw his role as a teacher: "Our job is as guides to help them find the little steps that they can take to end the huge problems." One of his students did a project about gang violence and found ways to facilitate dialogue in the community. He and other students held a peace circle with police and local youth. They explored conflict resolution and restorative justice and did a peace workshop with younger children where they considered together: "What does a culture of peace look like?" While this work was done one-on-one, the understandings that the students took away went beyond their immediate community. Students worked locally with different groups that experienced conflict and gained a new view of how they might act in their community (personal communication, April 2010).

"You need to have it so they engage in their own terms."

Framing world problems within a local context may give students opportunity to become more effective at adjusting big questions to their capabilities—that is, local is more chewable than global! "Students must not get lost in the complexity of the world, nor become simply rooted in compassion for it," says Zimmerman. "They must have some measure of control or power within themselves to effect the changes they [come to] understand are needed" (2004, p. 4). Thus, first-graders might grow, pick, wash, and weigh pumpkins and then deliver them to a food kitchen while middle-schoolers might become involved in a construction project at a new homeless shelter. They could build, consult with designers, seek out funding to furnish the shelter, and contribute artwork to the final building.

High school students might work with people living at a shelter and their neighbors on a community mural and hold public conversations on how people treat each other.

Students can surprise grown-ups in terms of what they can accomplish. We need to refrain from overloading a young person's learning agenda, yet we also need to think about the dangers of expecting too little. In the same way that Ellen chooses to read and produce Shakespeare plays with fifth-graders, much to the amazement of parents and colleagues, *we need to be vigilantly open to students' untapped possibilities.* We cannot raise adults who are able to tackle the complexity of modern life unless they have the opportunity, in safe and authentic ways, to grapple with real challenges in communities.

> *"There isn't one way for all kids . . . everyone has to determine their way in."*

Organizing service opportunities poses a much more complex view of curriculum. Does one require it? Assign it? One teacher notes, "I would rather show them the possibilities and then they find something to do on their own. I'm a little uncomfortable with volunteering kids." Service challenges us to be vigilant to the needs and moral growth of our students. The outcomes move beyond what is usually accepted as "regular school work." Messing about in real problems requires the teacher to be deeply attuned to the needs, readiness, and unexpressed potential of the students.

When teachers learn to bridge from basic skills and traditional content to larger purposes, assessment gains an authenticity not present in simulated "problems." Assessment becomes more of a human conversation about doing good work.

Authentic Assessment and Shared Purpose

> "There is, I think, no point in the philosophy of progressive education which is sounder than its emphasis upon the importance of the participation of the learner in the formation of the purposes which direct . . . the learning process, just as there is no defect in traditional education greater than its failure to secure the active co-operation of the pupil in construction of the purposes involved in . . . studying."
>
> *John Dewey (1938, p. 67)*

Part of the beauty of that spring day at the pond with my students was that it was a shared learning experience. I wasn't telling them what to do or recording the number of questions they asked or asking them to summarize their findings, although I could do all of those things in a different context. We were just learning together, experiencing a pond in springtime. We shared the discovery, the wonder, and the fun! Not all inquiry is that spontaneous, nor does it have to be messy, but the effusive energy at the pond suggests this "active co-operation" (see previous quote) makes assessment more authentic.

Cara Cabler, a Vermont teacher, noticed this "active cooperation" when her students had to present their plan to the city in order to build a skate park:

> This was truly authentic learning: students cared about the research and how the presentation looked, we presented to a real audience, we involved members of the community, we looked to people for answers (not books) and students gained skills they will use later in life.
>
> *(quoted in Demarest, 2008, p. 10)*

Learners can feel when they are being asked to do something worthwhile. The bait of "success in the future," "scoring well on tests," and "getting a job later on" rings hollow for most students. Students will respond more to "this is interesting, challenging, and fun—right now!" When students are given a chance to set their own goals and choose their own path, they are cognitively and emotionally committed. This is how the term "learning journey" is used when describing personalized learning. There is a commitment from the learner to keep going toward the outcome.

In inquiry-based learning, students can become part of the assessment process and design, assess, and track criteria in a way that has meaning; it is not just a task on a rubric. The authenticity of an assessment process rests on the student's participation in setting and implementing goals as well as determining their worth and progress. A conversation about assessment can start with the four elements of local learning:

- What did this mean to you?
- What knowledge did you gain?
- What new understanding of your local place do you now have?
- What understanding of your role in working with others (present and future) do you now have?

Real work is felt in the community; authentic outcomes can impact peoples' lives. People become vested in the learning when they act as "sources" sharing possible answers to the questions. In the process, they change their thinking about youth and schools.

Authentic Assessment Involves Establishing Criteria before and during the Work

Learning to ask good questions, pose possible answers, organize material, and analyze findings are among the many skills students need in order to be successful at inquiry. Good teachers manage to ensure there is timely and valuable feedback on all parts of the process (although feedback does not always come from the teacher). Teacher and students engage in a form of task analysis to learn what skills are necessary to solve the problem. As one teacher put it, *"It takes a lot more for students to work through it, but if I am paying attention to what they are asking, we can usually figure out what they need to get done."*

When students come together on a question, they begin the work. This demands a certain level of comfort with not knowing all the answers or having a detailed plan. While many traditional skills and knowledge remain important, new skills emerge. One teacher was surprised when she found herself coaching her students on how to make a telephone call, an important first step when interviewing someone. Learning to introduce yourself, state your purpose, and obtain and record the needed information becomes a valued skill. Another teacher might find herself helping a student learn to use a hoe or a hammer.

If students design an investigation where they use their talents, learn new things, and work with other students and people outside of school, they have gone a long way to developing criteria of value on which they can be assessed. Such a list can become a checklist from which students plan and reflect on their progress and get feedback from peers, the teacher, and other adults. Together, teachers and students can describe what they are aiming for without knowing exactly what it looks like when they start. They learn to follow the work.

> *"They have to put the whole puzzle together . . . not just*
> *a little piece."*

A teacher can be explicit in teaching and assessing specific skills. Often the skills are recognized ("you will need to gather information from your parents on what this street used to look like") and implemented ("include the quotes from your interviewees in your PowerPoint") but not assessed on the final assessment. The assessment tool might only include "organization, clarity, and creativity" and not "depth of questions, variety of perspectives, or tenacity in following up with neighbors." New learning might be shared at a community event and challenge students to use communication skills, empathy, and patience. The student deserves ongoing feedback on these new skills.

Authentic Assessment Involves Active Reflection

Reflection is used to deepen learning by establishing personal threads of meaning. Intentionally including time for active reflection alongside new knowledge, skills, and experiences requires a lot of "space" in the curriculum. Journals, research papers, blogs, and dialogue all give students time to think. The teacher creates room for a response to the questions, *"What does this mean to me?"* and *"How will this learning take me somewhere new?"* A high school student reflects:

"I think my strengths as a researcher are typical for my age. I think the first time I did a major research project was in middle school. I did mess up a lot, but I learned from my mistakes. I slowly evolved from less mistakes and less errors. I am used to doing projects that are scientifical [*sic*], but this project I had to interview people and that was something new for me. The way past projects were . . . you could just find answers on the Internet, but this one you had to find the answers from other peoples' knowledge and their opinion. So a difficult challenge for me was interviewing. . . . My partner helped me get comfortable and relaxed . . . and he let me ask questions when I felt comfortable enough to ask. I think this research project helped me move up on to the next stage."

"When they're talking more and figuring things out—that is the basis for reflection."

Reflection is an active process. Although it is often viewed as a quiet, solitary activity, reflection can be noisy and shared. It can be a short "pair and share" or a five-minute journal entry or a large public portfolio of learning assembled after a learning experience. It involves actively digging in, "using it" as Kate phrased it, and sorting out its significance before proceeding to the next task. Reflection helps students internalize the work. In authentic assessment, students learn to track their progress on a wide spectrum of achievement from illustrating a millipede to an act of service.

****

When considering curriculum, a teacher will ask: *What are our questions? What do we need to learn in order to find answers? How should we communicate what we learned?* Teachers who want their students to be more engaged find ways to share ownership of the decisions that drive the curriculum. Sometimes this is simply making the purpose more transparent. Gay comments, "When it's not a new project every time they walk in the door . . . being able to come in and know exactly what they are going to do because they have already started it . . . they do value that." Another middle school teacher comments, "I didn't realize how little I shared with [my students] what I hoped we could accomplish. You need to take the time to talk about your goals and see what they think. How else can they be truly involved?"

"It's about building a community—over time we learn about each other, and then we use that."

When there is a shared purpose of "this is what we are about," there is an ethos of "knowledge seekers," a hum to the enterprise. Pursuing a wide range of questions about issues and themes that naturally emerge from the places where we live gives students compelling reasons to learn and grow.

Making space for this work is an organic process; a teacher does not decide to change overnight. Once you invite the millipede into the classroom, you find yourself paying more and more attention to it. When teachers use the local environment as a vehicle for engaging students in the educational enterprise, a multitude of changes take place within the traditional relationships between teacher, student, and knowledge. These changes involve interrelated layers of decisions and choices during which the teacher comes to see students' learning differently, discovers new ways to teach, and comes to see her role as teacher, the capacity of their students, and the reasons for learning in a new light.

★★★★★★★★★★

References

Boggs, J., & Boggs, G. L. (1974). *Revolution and evolution in the twentieth century*. New York, NY: Monthly Review Press.

Chittenden, E. (2005). What is taught, what is learned. In B. S. Engel with A. C. Martin (Eds.), *Holding values: What we mean by progressive education* (pp. 160–164). Portsmouth, NH: Heinemann.

Demarest, A. B. (2008). *Shared purpose: How teachers engage the local environment and community to design meaningful and democratic curriculum* (Doctoral dissertation). College of Education and Social Services, University of Vermont, Burlington.

Dewey, J. (1902). The child and the curriculum. In R. D. Archambault (Ed.), *John Dewey on education: Selected writings* (pp. 339–358). Chicago, IL: University of Chicago Press.

Dewey, J. (1922). The nature of aims. In R. D. Archambault (Ed.), *John Dewey on education: Selected writings* (pp. 70–80). Chicago, IL: University of Chicago Press.

Dewey, J. (1938). *Experience and education*. New York, NY: Macmillan.

Geography Education Standards Project. (1994). *Geography for life: The national geography standards*. Washington, DC: National Geographic Society Committee on Research and Exploration.

Sobel, D. (1996). *Beyond ecophobia: Reclaiming the heart in nature education* (1st ed.). Great Barrington, MA: The Orion Society.

Wiggins, G., & McTighe, J. (1998). *Understanding by design* (1st ed.). Alexandria, VA: Association for Supervision and Curriculum Development.

Wiggins, G., & McTighe, J. (2013). *Essential questions: Opening doors to student understanding*. Alexandria, VA: Association for Supervision and Curriculum Development.

Zimmerman, E. (2004). Educating for sustainability: Actors in the web of community. *Community Works Journal, 6*(3), 4, 45.

PART II

Elements of Place-based Curriculum Design

Purpose and Function

The rich, experiential, open-ended nature of local learning can cause confusion in a world that continually asks for clear, measurable outcomes. This seeming lack of clarity can cloud curricular intentions and often relegates the more authentic experiences out of mainstream curriculum design. Identifying the fundamental elements of this practice enables us to better communicate our curricular purpose regarding planning and assessment in dialogue with colleagues, parents, students, and the larger community. This chapter looks systematically at the curricular elements of local learning.

"A palette of possibilities."

It has struck me in my own work and research that there are four recognizable, not entirely distinct, curricular elements that teachers use when they *engage the local*. Just as there are three primary colors that make up the rainbow of possible colors in this world, identifying these four approaches shows the essential aspects of organizing community-based curriculum. In the same way that artists rarely use just pure red, blue, and yellow to create a work of art, a teacher seldom uses these approaches in their pure form. Yet the artist, in order to paint the many hues that make up our world, knows how the primary colors behave. These four approaches comprise the palette of possibilities with which teachers create the many ways students experience local learning.

Part II has four chapters. Each chapter presents one of these four elemental approaches and examines its structure and function. Examining each element separately presents a *palette* of colors teachers can consider as they design curriculum. Even though it is a complex and fluid undertaking, teachers who "paint with these colors" can be clear about how they structure what is being learned and how a study relates to school subjects—the assumed "business" of school. In doing so, they can better track subject mastery and specific skills as well as the larger out-comes that frame this work.

"The beauty is in the mix."

The boundaries between these four types of approaches are not fixed, and the ways teachers build connections to the local are much more organic than a neat diagram of identified elements suggests. While it is helpful to consider their function sepa-rately to illustrate the palette's color spectrum, artists rarely use only "red, blue, or yellow." It is equally informative to consider how they work in different combina-tions for different purposes. Indeed, the worth of naming the elements is more to appreciate the complexity of how a teacher creates "works of art" that blend the boundaries between "colors."

For example, food has gained a vital presence in some schools' curricula. A topic long relegated to nutrition class, food has become what some call a national movement or "revolution." There are now thousands of food-related programs sprouting up around the country (www.farmtoschool.org). Is it science? History? Civics? What pieces might a teacher weave together for young people to better understand the sources, pleasure, and benefits of healthy food? Students cook, learn where food comes from, and think about healthy choices. They learn how to transplant, irrigate, prune, and nurture food to make it grow, and they learn how to harvest and store root vegetables.

> "A significant part of the pleasure of eating is one's accurate consciousness of the lives and the world from which food comes."
> Wendell Berry (2009, p. 234)

While an initial attempt to grow food with students may come from an enthu-siastic feeling of "I want my students to have a garden," the teacher can view a clearer direction for the study as it grows. Does she want her students to have the *experience* of a garden, to learn from it *scientific principles,* to understand how *people in the community* have gardened over time, or to *impact the local food system?* The ways students experience their local community is rarely contained within traditional subject-based boundaries. Cognitive references to the real world happen all the time, no matter how carefully the teacher anticipates the outcomes. Communally shared experience might result in learning that:

- resonates with students' past experiences,
- deepens an understanding of a single subject,
- compels a connection from one subject to another, or
- provides a deeper connection to self through service or critical questioning.

Outlining the elements in this way accommodates the many ways to frame curriculum. The subject area might have different weight and relevance, student engagement will always vary, and the outcome as envisioned by the teacher might shift. My choice of circles to represent the interplay and prominence of place, subject, and student voice echoes the work of James Beane (1997) who provides a helpful distinction between interdisciplinary, multidisciplinary, and integrated curriculum used in this book. A teacher may frame a study with one purpose in mind but have it transform into another unanticipated experience entirely. Classrooms (and communities!) are the studios for how each work of art is created. There is no one way. Like art, it is a creative process.

Curricular Elements of Local Learning

PERSONAL CONNECTIONS ARE THE FOUNDATION OF ALL LEARNING
How can I better relate school to my students' life experiences?

Teachers use local places and past experiences to deepen cognitive and emotional connections to what is being learned. Often, not a formal curriculum undertaking, this approach reflects the use of ongoing connections students build from the questions they have about the places where they live and relate to their past, present, and future experiences.

LOCAL INVESTIGATIONS DEEPEN SUBJECT UNDERSTANDING
How can I help students better understand how this big idea works in the real world?

Teachers make use of the many ways places offer firsthand evidence of content and concepts of school subjects that occur in local places. Students explore "BIG IDEAS" that are manifest in the local landscape and have the opportunity to question, validate, and affirm understanding of key concepts. The real world acts as a curricular laboratory to deepen students' understanding of content.

LOCAL INVESTIGATIONS BUILD HOLISTIC UNDERSTANDING OF PLACES
How can I help students better understand this place?

Teachers pose questions about local places as organizing themes for students to learn about the places where they live. The character, history, details, and needs of a place emerge as students explore the "stories of places" through a multidisciplinary or an interdisciplinary lens. The stories they uncover may combine subjects in different ways that reflect the complexity of places, but the emphasis remains on understanding the place.

LOCAL INVESTIGATIONS BUILD OPPORTUNITY FOR CIVIC ENGAGEMENT
How can I help students better understand themselves and their possible futures?

The teacher creates space for the student—in partnership with community members—to generate, explore, and address problems and issues that plague society. Subjects are mastered in the contexts of work done pursuing answers to students' questions. The teacher has not mapped out the direction or outcome of these inquiries; rather, they emerge from the work students do. This work alters traditional views of schoolwork and offers the student a new level of engagement and possibility.

FIGURE 3.1

Amy B. Demarest, Place-based Curriculum Design: Exceeding Standards through Local Investigations. © Routledge, 2015.

TEACHER PORTRAIT #2
SHARYL GREEN
ELEMENTARY

"Part of my responsibility is to honor all questions."

Hearing the chatter and excitement through the trees, I came to where Sharyl's third-grade students were building their shelters. This day was one of the last that they would spend learning from this tract of land that had provided a year's worth of questions and answers about moss, stone walls, and more. Today the agenda was play, a deep kind of play that matched the beauty of the tall pine forest. Working with hand saws, under the watchful eye of parent volunteers, they were building shelters on the land. One group had decorated a hearth with stones that they were hauling into the lean-to. Another group had created a mobile of sticks and leaves to dangle from their entrance. The following week they would return for a celebratory sleepover in the shelters they had built.

The school where Sharyl teaches in rural Vermont is near the village. The parking lot abuts a horse paddock, so you are sometimes greeted by a large workhorse peering over the fence when you arrive. Although the scene appears tranquil and the school enjoys a good deal of parent support, the district recently faced a strike vote and installed a locked front door with a buzz-in system—as many schools in the country have done. Sharyl has a playful and warm teaching style. On her Aunt Hazel's 100th birthday, students made cards and had to find some way of representing 100 to include in the card. She is a veteran of 30 plus years and well-practiced at her craft. However, it is her openness to new learning—a phrase she uses to describe her most cherished outcome for her students—that makes her the artist that she is.

In the yearlong study that focuses on a nearby stretch of preserved fields, wood, and stream, students explore their questions. The land serves as a hearth for independent research and inquiry as students address subject standards, become familiar with a piece of land in their town, and form a question that they would like to answer. The culminating event of this study involves creating a brochure about their research. The final brochures, complete with illustrations, quotes, and relevant data, are available at the town library for residents to learn more about the land's history, wildlife, ecosystem interrelationships, and other natural phenomena.

The process of brochure design is a complex one, inspired by the goal that their work will be used to educate their neighbors. The task involves deep and prolonged inquiry in which each child is given time to develop a research question that is personally significant. Students are required to find local experts on their topic and use them as sources in addition to printed text.

Sharyl reflects, "We encourage students to figure out what they are most curious about in this outdoor classroom where we hike, write, map, experiment and listen to guest speakers . . . it is now a tradition."

3

PERSONAL CONNECTIONS ARE THE FOUNDATION OF ALL LEARNING

"The school must represent life—life as real and vital to the child as that which he carries on in the home, in the neighborhood, or on the playground."

John Dewey (1897, p. 430)

PERSONAL CONNECTIONS ARE THE FOUNDATION OF ALL LEARNING	
How can I better relate school to my students' life experience?	
	Teachers use local places and past experiences to deepen cognitive and emotional connections to what is being learned. Often, not a formal curriculum undertaking, this approach reflects the use of ongoing connections students build from the questions they have about the places where they live and relate to their past, present, and future experiences.

FIGURE 3.2

Amy B. Demarest, Place-based Curriculum Design: Exceeding Standards through Local Investigations. © Routledge, 2015.

The need to make learning a more relevant experience is endorsed daily by the numbers of American students who "vote with their feet" to disengage or drop out of school. For many, the bland menu of curricular offerings fails to engage them on a personal, emotional, or spiritual level. While policy pundits carry on about high achievement, students are searching for a spark of human interest in the schoolhouse. This chapter examines the many ways a student's life experiences influence the nature and quality of the learning time spent in school (see Figure 3.2).

Considering local learning from this perspective acknowledges the wisdom of the "anticipatory set" or "hook" that advises teachers to seek an initial cognitive spark to get students involved. It is not so much about the standard as getting ready for the standard. One spring, in anticipation of a unit on interdependence, when students would be studying insects, birds, and habitats on a global scale, I assigned a bird watch as the weather was warming. I asked students to look out for different kinds of birds as they arrived in northern Vermont. No credit, no grades, just an invitation. *"Blue Jays! Cardinals! I saw this little yellow bird this morning but I don't know what it was. You should have seen the size of that crow!"* Every morning, I was stampeded by an unleashed birding energy as we recorded sightings on a chart. What they saw primed them to consider migration and global interdependence with "new eyes."

Experience is the impetus for all education. The phenomenon of learning is an active process and involves a change in thinking in the mind of the learner. To learn, students need a personal incentive to connect their existing ideas and perceptions to new information. While this is fundamental to all teaching, it is a distinct way teachers use local investigations.

Experience Is the Foundation of Learning

When I visited the Martin Luther King Middle School in Berkeley, California, a class of sixth-graders was making homegrown pizza and cooking it in a wood-fired oven that sat next to their garden. They used the tomatoes and other veggies to make the sauce. What was most impressive about this endeavor was not the beautifully tended garden or the quantities of food that spilled from it, but the energy that was generated around the meal. In the Kitchen Classroom, students set tables with tablecloths, made lemonade from the nearby lemon tree, and created a centerpiece of freshly cut flowers. When everything was ready, we all gathered at the different tables with the expectation that we would engage in friendly conversation—dinner table talk . . . slow food. I spoke with a young man who was bursting with pride as he described how he cooked most of the meals for his family—three siblings and his mother: "My moms likes just about everything I fix—and she likes it when I have dinner ready when she comes home from work." A teacher reflecting on the happy energy of the day as we cleaned up said, "Students smile more when they are in the garden . . . why aren't we doing more things that make kids smile?"

"Making it relevant is a lot about making it local."

This element is the foundation on which the big ideas of the standards can come alive. It is the canvas on which art is created! A math teacher might refer to how fractions are used in recipes, a language arts teacher could ask students to think about love and loss while reading Shakespeare, or an art teacher could ask her students to draw bicycles instead of flower vases. Ongoing connections to the world outside the classroom are already at work in students' thinking and can be used to make school a more authentic experience.

> "When place is incorporated into the act of curriculum development, children's everyday experiences become one of the foundations upon which learning is constructed."
>
> Greg Smith (2013, p. 213)

Teachers who seek to bridge their content to the social and emotional world of their students ground the learning experience in what students know and who they are. Dewey explains the physiological rationale of this allegiance when he describes that "learning is active. It involves the reaching out of the mind . . . the organic assimilation starting from within. Literally we must *take our stand* [emphasis added] with the child and our departure from him (Dewey, 1902, p. 343).

Taking a stand with the learner is about establishing a partnership that guides the educational process. Teachers can build an intellectual as well as a more personal, emotional bridge to the content that makes learning "very real, very right now." This view is both student-centered in terms of what the learner knows and thinks, as well as place-centered in terms of what the learner experiences.

Damion Mitchell. Used with permission.

Taking a stand also means to stand by the learner in terms of what is valuable and useful. New teachers are not asked to take a vow to never bore a student, to never teach information that is useless, outdated, or so far afield from the learner's experience that there is no way for the material to be processed. However, good teachers take their obligations to young people seriously because they know the many ways that learning *requires* an emotional connection. Posing academic questions in the abstract misses what students already *know* about their world, as well as how students feel about their world. Linking to students' emotions involves paying attention to the geographical places of students—in the very largest meaning of the word.

"I like live experiences. I feel like that's what works."

Paying attention to how students feel reflects a more empathetic view toward how students experience their education. It means that teachers should also attend to students' expressions of apathy. Schoolwork can become a small act of hope that gives a student a stronger sense of efficacy. Researching recipes to share at a food shelf, building a ramp, shoveling a sidewalk, or sharing a story all can ease a feeling of hopelessness. Attending to their concerns and questions makes it more likely that they will be engaged. Gay reflects:

> . . . after all, they are teenagers. It's all about them. They're so there. You know it's only going to stay with them any length of time if it's related to them. If it's not related to them it's in one ear and out the other. It doesn't even stop to rest.

Teachers Seek Connections to Student Experience

"If I fail to make that connection, then I lose them more often than not."

Ellen states that providing a concrete connection is key: "When you can use the places they've seen . . . it draws on their experience and their fund of information so that they can make connections to the bigger ideas. . . . It's because of this connection that they have to make sense of it." She says she works to make these "connections in writing, in reading, and across the board as much as I can." Ellen reflects that even though we offer the connections to deepen learning, it does not mean that the process is easier for students: "It actually makes it harder because they have to resolve what they know with new information." When Jean seeks to "deepen the connection," he asks, "How can I reach out to where kids come from and their experiences to enrich the particular curriculum?":

> Things become less abstract. Meaning is more rich. I think that students find more interest, because it's not something that happened a long time ago or far away or in a theoretical sense. But it's happening . . . [it] has relevance to the environment today.

Jean maintains ways that a student's personal connection to the material underlines the worth of any intellectual inquiry: "Here's Mesopotamia and what happened there—devoid of a connection to self—what is the value in that? History helps us understand who we are and who we're not." In framing a more critical view, Jean wants his students to ask the big questions that he feels frame the study of history and prompts students to inquire: "What questions aren't being asked? What's not being told? Whose voice is not being heard?"

Steven Schmidt. Used with permission.

When I first started teaching about the Lake Champlain Basin, I was bowled over by the many personal connections that students had to the lake where most of them had grown up. It was an unanticipated energy that poured into the classroom, and, as a new teacher, I found it exciting—and a complication! For any "lesson" undertaken, there was a childhood memory, a relative, a memorable bike ride, and other experiences that a student retrieved to enrich our understanding of the topic. These vibrant connections were a bridge back home; students more often shared their learning with family members and neighbors, coming up with a better answer to the question, *What did you do in school today?*

"When they don't care about it, they don't learn it."

I once gave a guest presentation on reading strategies to a fifth-grade class using a selection from *Wind in the Willows*. A student asked a question that made me realize I had glossed over the title of the book assuming it was familiar to them. I backed up and showed them the cover, and, all of a sudden, a boy who had been sitting in the back of the room with his arms crossed jumped up and exclaimed: "My grandma has a willow tree in her backyard." This connection totally changed his attitude, and he actively took part for the rest of the lesson. While his experience with willow trees did not lend itself directly to the lesson underway, it did offer him a genuine reason to connect. Students always need a reason, and the local context provides so many.

One way that teachers can connect to students' lives outside of school is to inquire into their experience of work. Do they have jobs at home or in the workplace? What values and skills do they use in work that can be useful in school? While many links to work are formalized (school-to-work, internships, and career building), there is a value in informally integrating students' experience of work. It might be a discussion of chores done at home or an artistic exploration of what worthwhile work looks like. Students of any age may be proud of the trust their family puts in them to cook, clean, take care of siblings, hunt, or care for an elder. Older students, many of whom have jobs, may excel at their work and not be able to transfer this success at school. Teachers can tap into their feelings of pride and competence.

Honoring Diverse Experience

Due to the varied background of our students and their constant need for connections, common experience becomes a critical foundation for learning and fundamental to creating community. How students filter, perceive, and experience their lived environment comes in to play when they learn. I once had a student whose family was not able to take him to many cultural or educational events, but he watched a lot of science programs on television. He regularly contributed important background information from a very impressive bank of scientific knowledge. As a learner, he sought ways to make sense of new material in relation to what he already knew, which, for him, was gathered from television.

> "We must look unblinkingly at the way children really are, and struggle to make sense of everything that we see in order to teach them."
>
> William Ayers (2001, p. 33)

Teachers need to stop and ask: "What different assumptions are students bringing to this material that warrant closer examination?" and "What do we need to know together as common context?" When teachers turn to their community, they realize the importance of this common experience.

"We become a community by the nature of the work that we do."

Local learning has the potential to be more inclusive. Investigations that are collaborative in nature invite the sharing of stories. Students from varied backgrounds all benefit from experiencing questions together. Learning can revolve around these *common reference points*. If students have traveled from another country, these experiences become the cornerstone of a growing understanding of where they now live. The stories and experiences they bring with them can be part of the narrative they use to build awareness of their new home.

Issues discussed in class resonate differently for students with diverse life experiences. If a teacher is not familiar with the background of her students, not only may she be insensitive, she might also miss an opportunity to use student experiences as a bridge to deepen learning. When Kate asks the question "what is war?" she includes the experience of her students who come from war-torn countries. She asks "How can you talk about Civil War and not acknowledge that [war] is a huge part of some students' lives?" She believes that their collective experiences need to be shared in order to build a learning community. The strength of this community becomes critical when students can share painful realities.

****

When students are immersed in local learning, they constantly have points of intersection with what they already know, where their learning is either affirmed or questioned. When teachers open up the classroom to the complicated lives of students, they need to be ready for the questions that emerge. In an iterative process, the student refers new knowledge to the world that is familiar. While not always linked to specific subjects or organized as formal curriculum, the ways that teachers seek to link learning to a student's existing knowledge, experience, and emotional world are essential aspects to learning in a local context. The next approach to structuring curriculum describes ways that teachers intentionally seek to deepen content acquisition and formally organize it as curricular goals.

****

References

Ayers, W. (2001). *To teach: The journey of a teacher.* New York, NY: Teachers College Press.

Beane, J. (1997). *Curriculum integration: Designing the core of democratic education.* New York, NY: Teachers College Press.

Berry, W. (2009). *Bringing it to the table: On farming and food.* Berkeley, CA: Counterpoint.

Dewey, J. (1897). My pedagogic creed. In R. D. Archambault (Ed.), *John Dewey on education: Selected writings* (pp. 427–439). Chicago, IL: University of Chicago Press.

Dewey, J. (1902). The child and the curriculum. In R. D. Archambault (Ed.), *John Dewey on education: Selected writings* (pp. 339–358). Chicago, IL: University of Chicago Press.

Smith, G. (2013). Place-based education: Practice and impacts. In R. B. Stevenson, M. Brody, J. Dillon, & A. E. J. Wals (Eds.), *International handbook on environmental education* (pp. 213–220). New York, NY: Routledge.

TEACHER PORTRAIT #3

GAY CRAIG

HIGH SCHOOL

"Absolutely, you've got to let them jump in the river."

Gay's study of "Our River" is incorporated into the ecology unit that she has taught for 15 years. It's now a tradition and a regular part of the curriculum and has earned solid community and administrative support. "We look at rivers in Montana, and those are very cool, but they're not our river . . . [in which] they're so much more interested. They call it 'our river' and years later and want to know what's going on in the river, how many macroinvertebrates there are. [They] compare siblings' findings to theirs . . . Is that my sister's result? Is that what her class got?" They want to find out, and they want to go home and tell people what they found out.

Gay's passion for learning in the field is palpable: "I've been testing water [for 30 years]. I think it's because I love to be outdoors myself, and kids do. I mean we would be outdoors every day if they had their way and I had my way, but we can't be. So when we can we love it. We love it."

"There's nothing more exciting than when a kid comes up to you with their calculator and their probe and is actually registering a number that is reasonable," she says. "[When it] fits into the water quality parameters—or they find calcium with the color comparator. Whoa. To them this is huge. They didn't have any idea there was calcium in that water, and there it was . . . it showed it. The color changed. They get very excited about it."

It is this excitement that she believes leads students to be stewards of the places they live. The big understanding she seeks is: "That's my water, and I want to take care of it." Gay stands behind the conviction to "Let kids be kids!" "Absolutely," she says. "You've got to let them jump in the river. You've got to let them try to beat each other jumping across the river, knowing that half of them are going to land in the middle." She tells the story of one family: "I've had two of the brothers; they did macro invertebrate testing. The third chose macro invertebrate testing, and they all fell in the river. His mother told me it's a family tradition. And they have one more brother coming."

Students share their data with local watershed organizations. "[Our work] goes into the big picture that way," says Gay. This fills her criteria for place-based education: "The location is local. The problem is local. There are groups in the community we work with. There is an outlet for us to share our data with the community. That is all you need for a place-based experience."

Gay says: "I've had kids come back years later and tell me about another river they lived near. They stay tuned in to what's happening. Now ask them about cell structure function? They don't remember a thing. Nothing. No one has ever come back and talked to me about that. But they come and talk to me about rivers and water quality. They send emails. They know it's important. It's there wherever you go."

4

LOCAL INVESTIGATIONS DEEPEN SUBJECT UNDERSTANDING

"Geometry didn't used to be a puzzle. Geometry was—as the name tells us—a way to measure land. We used the Pythagorean Theorem to set four corners in our pasture—of course we had no idea what it was. At school Geometry was mainly a puzzle, something to memorize for the test. But place-based education is not a puzzle or an abstraction. Teachers can use that fence post as a way to connect a concept with the real world. Isn't that what education is about?"

Jack Shelton (2006, p. 7)

LOCAL INVESTIGATIONS DEEPEN SUBJECT UNDERSTANDING	
How can I help students better understand how this big idea works in the real world?	
PLACE SUBJECT	Teachers make use of the many ways places offer firsthand evidence of content and concepts of school subjects that occur in local places. Students explore "BIG IDEAS" that are manifest in the local landscape and have the opportunity to question, validate, and affirm understanding of key concepts. The real world acts as a curricular laboratory to deepen students' understanding of content.

FIGURE 4.1

Amy B. Demarest, Place-based Curriculum Design: Exceeding Standards through Local Investigations. © Routledge, 2015.

A second element of how teachers structure local learning is to pursue a discipline- or multi-discipline-specific study related to a particular subject or subjects. The study is framed around an essential question posed by the subject. The teacher organizes formal learning that focuses on a local "answer." What may seem like a remote idea in a textbook becomes real when a student examines evidence of erosion in a river, interviews residents about an alternative form of energy, or observes the way a bee pollinates a flower. Students gain a deeper understanding of the subject by delving into its real-world manifestation outside the classroom. This chapter explores the way that the environment outside of the school building can provide a rich laboratory in which to investigate all subjects (see Figure 4.1).

"Big ideas help my student relate."

A local place offers firsthand experience of content and concepts that comprise the subjects we are required to teach. Teachers—and students—can identify the questions that naturally reside in local places. This "local investigation" involves a deeper involvement than just an experiential connection. These authentic explorations can reside in what is considered the "normal" work of school with well-designed field trips and forays into the community. A science teacher might use the local stream to teach river ecology, or a history and math teacher might collaborate with a social studies teacher to investigate architectural styles. The enhanced understanding of the subjects is the desired outcome.

Subjects Come Alive in Local Places

In this approach, the study of food would be more closely related to a subject. A teacher might be teaching about soil and find a way to have a local study that connects students to the school garden. A veteran seventh-grade science teacher and recent convert to using food as an organizing theme exclaims: "I can teach my whole science curriculum through our gardens!" Indeed, students can learn about plant growth, soil chemistry and soil health, environmental impacts, erosion, climate patterns, and the life cycle of worms. A social studies teacher might welcome the opportunity to study local food traditions, share family recipes, and explore new food ways that have arrived with recent immigrants. Students can create art that celebrates food and how it grows, write press releases about developments in the garden, and puzzle out the geometry of a new garden plan. Food can provide many varied single- or multi-subject-based learning opportunities.

Why Explore the Local Question?

I once visited a geology class to share some of the local story. One student exclaimed, "I never knew there was so much geology in Vermont!" Another student, in reference to Vermont's highest mountain that was literally in view from the classroom, exclaimed, "I never knew where Mt. Mansfield came from!" Their textbook had already "covered" many important principles of geologic change, but they had not had the opportunity to apply it to their own world. The use of the local gives deeper meaning to the place-less, generic packaging of knowledge so predominant in our schools. When teachers use this approach, they ask themselves and their students, "How do these big ideas, concepts, and events play out where we live?"

Another geology teacher designed a unit based on the essential question, *How does the earth's surface change?* She began the study by asking her students to investigate the evidence nearby to see how the earth's surface changed. Students discovered weathering, fission, and cracking and maintained this local thread throughout the unit as they learned about earth-moving forces around the globe. At the end of the unit, they were able to demonstrate their grasp of the essential question both globally and locally.

This approach illustrates an element of local studies that is foundational to designing place-based curriculum. Standards represent big ideas that explain how the world works. The way to see how the world works is to look outside. Teachers organize curriculum based on big ideas and incorporate investigations of the local community. Rather than reading about what others have found out (although they do that too), students are acting more like historians, scientists, writers, and mathematicians to uncover their own answers to the big questions. This view is celebrated by a pre-school teacher who said: "I want to teach them about the sun's effect on the earth's temperature while they are down on the ground—so they can think with their brains while on their belly feeling the coolness of the earth."

Brandon Cohen. Used with permission.

In all subjects, teachers can ground their students' questions in the local community and "test" the more abstract claims of a textbook when they ask: *"How does it play out in my community? What actually happens in the real world?"* A teacher can saturate her study of global climates all year long by frequent forays outside. Students can collect local data by observing plant growth, leaf behavior, animal signs, and the sky. She can ask: *What is happening? What evidence of spring do you see? Why did the pond dry up? Is this photosynthesis? What do birds do in the winter?* The following chart shows how traditional subject-based questions can shift with a local focus:

SUBJECT-DISTINCT ESSENTIAL QUESTIONS SHIFT TO PLACE-BASED

How do birds survive?	⟶ What do our birds need to survive?
What is ecology?	⟶ Is our local pond an ecosystem?
What is democracy?	⟶ How does our city council make decisions?
What is history?	⟶ Who are the history-makers in this place?
What are mathematical patterns?	⟶ What mathematical patterns are found in nature?
What is interdependence?	⟶ How are animals in the back woods interconnected?
How does the surface of the earth change?	⟶ How was this land formed?
What is art?	⟶ How do people around here express themselves?

Teachers can provoke students to examine their environment to see if things really happen a certain way. For example, while learning about photosynthesis, teachers can ask students to consider: *What evidence do you see that this is how plants grow? Does it really happen this way? Would you change this description of (plant growth) if you were writing this text?* Students can examine rock formation, weather patterns, and human settlement and transportation patterns. One teacher wanted to address the attributes of plants by learning about how they grew near school. She pursued the question, "What is a plant?" She posed a problem to her students and asked them to prove that what was growing nearby were plants that needed active protection and provided certain benefits to the community. A teacher doesn't need a park nearby to ask these questions. Plants behave as plants in different settings—on a windowsill, pushing up through concrete, or in a patch of woods.

When Ellen teaches the water curriculum that is required by her district, she finds ways to incorporate local learning. Field trips, water poems, scientific observations, and local maps all augment the general topics presented in the textbook. In one of those serendipitous, but still unwelcome, moments of teaching, her town experienced significant spring flooding. Students understood how a river could overflow its banks when they saw the drenched fields on the way to school. The natural phenomena of flooding "proved" what was in the textbook and gave students an appreciation for the power of water when they saw the overturned trailer that had tumbled into a cornfield. A student commented: "Local things can help you understand it better. [...] If teachers were just trying to describe it, we wouldn't have a really good idea what it was. But giving us something that we know and see every day, it's easier to understand what it is." Their understanding at the end of the unit was not limited to local rivers and streams; their grasp of how water behaves globally was enhanced by local investigations.

> "For children, developing a relationship with our big planet comes from small, specific encounters. We see, smell and touch the shelf fungus decomposing a fallen log and see a flower springing from the enriched soil—and we understand the cycle of life and death. We watch a hawk circle, dive, and flap off with a struggling snake—and the thrill we feel embeds the concept of energy flow in our minds and our guts. We sit in silence and listen to a brook trickle by, our own breath joining the breeze, and we feel connected to a place and a planet. Developing a relationship with a place that encompasses our minds, hearts and bodies is what place-based learning is all about."
>
> Cindy Jenson-Elliott (2011, pp. 9–10)

Sometimes a local study is organized as a "sidebar" to the main subject. The local investigation, taught alongside a traditional text or sequence, fuels the study and offers students a way to ground their learning. A teacher can use any subject-based text and add a local story. An ecology teacher can augment a study with visits to different habitats; a history teacher can study the Vietnam War and inquire into the local stories or study the Industrial Revolution and visit the local historical society. This might not qualify as a fully fledged place-based study as described in the next chapter, but it offers students a real-world corollary. In this approach, the subject is still the main concern and determines the structure. Teachers can offer the macro/micro in many different ways: the general/specific, the national/local, and the global/local.

Local Learning Builds Global Understanding

Subject-based local studies can build global understanding when students learn about local parts to a global whole. There are three different ways it is helpful to see subject-based local studies in relation to understanding our larger world.

Local learning builds understanding of a place far away

A basic curricular construct for a local study is "my place, your place, all places." In order to better understand a concept or an idea, a student can begin locally with "my place." Then the investigation of a place far away—"your place"—is better understood, and the student can come to understand how things work in "all places" with new eyes. *My river, your river, all rivers. My city, your city, all cities.*

When approaching new subject matter, students seek reference points to what they know. If the new learning is about something far away, teachers can compare it to what is nearby. We ask students to research a country or a faraway region and collect information in categories such as the economics, traditions, transportation, and food—without having any understanding of what these distinctions mean. Teachers can begin a global study by exploring concepts locally. *What are our traditions? Where does our food come from?* When it is time to study the place far away, students will have a more tangible comprehension of the concepts and be more effective researchers.

A second-grade teacher charged with teaching her students "Regions of the US" was pondering how abstract a place 3,000 miles wide was to an eight-year-old. We talked about how her students could first research the geographic, scientific, and literary terms that characterized where they lived and then learn about more distant and diverse regions of the United States. Fiction and nonfiction texts, maps, and images were all used as sources. In interpreting the different texts, the teacher asked: "What evidence do you find that this may have happened in the Midwest? What makes you think this story took place near the Rocky Mountains? Why are you so sure this poem is about a desert?" The culminating activity was a mural of artwork in which the students represented the diverse landscape, climate, natural resources, and lifestyles of each region. A rich mix of text, inquiry, and local touchstones helped her students grasp these questions and create evidence-based artifacts that showed the diversity of the regions.

A cultural exchange can take something (art, data sharing, stories, or action) of one place to another. Any project that asks students to look closely at their own

Doria Anselmo, Outside the Lens. Used with Permission

places can be used to share data with young people in other places. Quality of life, insect population, water quality, or any new learning can be shared. The student is expert on one thing and can get a more global perspective by sharing it. Use of Skype and other data-sharing technologies can facilitate this process.

Local learning can build global friendship. When students bring along an understanding of their own place in instances of cross-cultural exchange, the worth of the experience deepens. Such a program called "Outside the Lens: Picture Me, Picture You" (Cribbs, Newman, & Even, 2009) fosters communication between youth in California and Tanzania.

Local learning builds understanding of complex global issues

Globalization is a phenomenon written about in many different contexts, but how can young people best come to understand it? Rachel Wood, a high school social studies teacher in Vermont, created a place-based study of globalization in her 12th-grade humanities class. After readings and discussions to build an initial definition of the term, she asked her students to get outside and do what geographers do: ask people questions. In her assignment, Wood (2012) writes:

> Until now you have spent the semester researching the far-off places of our world: Latin America, the Middle East, Asia and Africa. You've explored maps and statistics on the internet, read and discussed a variety of texts, and critically analyzed film. While your research has been thorough, it hasn't been enough. In the coming weeks you will become a human geographer. Your community will become your classroom and you will direct your questions to real people, both familiar faces and new. Some questions might be …
> What are our connections to globalization?
> What are the places we interact with?
> What challenges are we facing as a community?
> What contrasts exist?

In teams and individually, students interviewed people who worked as cooks, factory workers, shopkeepers, car mechanics, truck drivers, and computer programmers to find out what globalization meant to people who lived and worked nearby. Zack Dustira investigated a company that makes T-shirts. His essay titled "Globalized Colors" is based on his interview with the vice president of a company that employs 175 employees in four different locations.

I am the vice president of the company and I have been working here since 1999. As this is a small Vermont business many roles require the wearing of multiple hats. My duties include the purchase of clothing we dye from our global venders, the selling and marketing of our product, call center supervising, and overseeing the manufacturing and distribution centers.

The company was founded in 1975 by Barry T. Chouinard. Our initial revenue came from contract dying other people's clothing. We would charge by the pound of clothing. In 1988, the company made a decision to stop dying other people's clothing and developed our own brand called "Comfort Colors." The brand has grown as has our small Vermont company's success.

I communicate with my vendors and customers via email and phone. When working on style changes, textile, or fabric issues we video chat with our global vendors. Much of our business happens over the Internet. Interaction with our global vendors is made very easy through Skype and other methods letting us connect like we are across town. Over 70% of our business is conducted through the Internet. Our business software allows us constant monitoring of all aspects of our business making us much more efficient.

Globalization has created this problem where we are now faced with longer lead times as more of our product is produced farther away, such as India, Pakistan, and China. The lesser developed countries where clothing is made struggle constantly with politics, power, environmental issues and human rights.

In America our youth does not have a desire to work factory jobs in cotton-dust filled textile plants. I have to run the company by the hand that was dealt by our government. The globalization we see in this industry comes from various trade agreements that constantly benefit us to move our production from one country to another. Outside of my job I personally disagree with a lot of what has happened through globalization. We have given away too many of our jobs in America (Colchester High School, 2012).

Wood, in considering the power of local inquiry, reflected:

This project excited my students in a way I've never seen before. 21st Century technologies have put the world at our fingertips, but there is only so much we can do from the classroom. This project is a full-body learning experience because students are truly immersed in globalization—not just reading about it. It requires that they pose real questions to real people, engage in authentic dialogue, and think critically about what they learn. Kids crave adult, real-world experience; they want to know that the work they are doing is valuable.

(personal communication, November 2, 2013)

Local learning provides opportunities to address global problems

A third way to consider local studies alongside global understanding is through service learning. Lindsey Halman, a teacher at the Edge Academy in Vermont, designed a unit on biodiversity and studied ecological issues and animal populations worldwide. Although the issue was first studied in a global context, she wanted her students to learn about threats to animals and successful conservation efforts that were happening locally. Using the question, "Who lives here?" she turned the lens (literally) to their suburban school campus and asked students to find out what was being done to improve the environment. Local wildlife experts helped them set up trail cameras to record animal activity near the school. Students researched animals such as squirrels and raccoons with the same rigor many other students learn about whales and tigers. When students were done with the unit, they educated others about their understanding of biodiversity globally as well as the local implications of the same issues.

Students who conduct authentic investigations in local places come to see the links between parts to a whole. Vermont students who addressed different energy issues and resources in their community and provided recommendations for alternative energy projects (Toolin & Watson, 2010) reported they were "motivated by their ability to ... discover the relevance of their projects to global and local energy issues" (p. 30). Students investigated topics such as hydroelectricity, alternative transportation, pellet heating systems, and the school's walk-in cooler to research solutions. One student was excited by the fact that "little changes could really add up and save a lot of money," and another felt her project helped to "make the world a better place on a small scale" (Toolin & Watson, 2010, p. 30).

> "The big problems of our world are going to be solved by groups of people working together in local places."
>
> Greg Smith (2007)

Climate change is certainly *the* global issue facing our youth, especially in communities ravaged by intense weather events. In many instances, it has become a grassroots effort with different people in the world working locally but communicating globally such as with 350.org. Students adjust their own lifestyle habits to changes that people all over the world are experiencing. While scientists and politicians argue over causes and solutions, young people can collect data, track climate changes, and take local action that gives them a sense of purpose. When climate-related disasters do strike, the ability to reach out with strategies for rebuilding is a way for young people to share a sense of community in a troubled world.

Authentic Practice of a Discipline

The essence of a discipline is richer, more rigorous, and more relevant than what often passes for science, social studies, writing, and mathematics in school. Teachers who use the local environment to explore subject matter seem to be dedicated to this more rigorous, authentic experience. They reflect on how they, themselves, learned to love their subject and want to share these powerful experiences with their students.

> *"I love nature and I want to share the wonder of it with my students."*

Science teachers have often been the first to employ the benefits of local study. Practicing real science outdoors is an incentive "to do what real scientists do." Gay took water samples for many years at her family's summer camp before she started teaching environmental science where she was able to meld her professional expertise with her personal passion. She says, "When I was able to teach about rivers and water quality, it was just like landing in heaven." Gay praised the benefits and joy of field experiences: "Being out there ... when you can see it instead of a picture. ... You're out there standing in the middle of the river.... . [It] doesn't get any better than that."

Teachers believe that local questions give students, as Ellen expresses it, "real reasons for reading, real reasons for writing, real reasons for talking to people, real reasons for finding out information ... these experiences [in the community] give them the real reasons." When Sharyl Green (see Teacher Portrait #2) voices her commitment to this way of teaching, she says it is because "the work is authentic" and that students have a way to pursue their own questions. In her view, this is how students experience "new learning."

> *"When they see it, they get it."*

For many of these teachers, this passion is their entry to local investigations. Ellen, a skilled teacher of writing, sought ways to have her students connect to what they knew and saw: " ... Now I want to do more. This is where it really happens." Teachers who intentionally use the local community to teach a subject do not do this as an aside; they believe it is the fuel for real learning.

Daniel Kriesberg (2000) offers an array of ways to consider how to observe nearby occurrences—to get "up close and personal" to scientific or human phenomenon. While his work focuses on trees, a similar approach can be used for a variety of local happenings and captures the idea of "my tree, your tree, all trees" central to this type of local studies. His study is of trees in the schoolyard (which is not an option for all schools), but nearby parks or one tree or other living things can be investigated. Kleisberg uses a sensory walk to start, homes in on observation and writing skills, and asks his students to read a variety of texts for research as well as literary portrayals of trees and treed landscapes in journals, fiction, and poetry. Students observe trees through the seasons, examine the life cycle of a tree, and map trees locally and in other places. Students find ways to publish their work and perform an act of service by planting trees in a nearby location.

A study like this illustrates both the learning content (what a tree does) and the practicing of the science (what a scientist does). It can be a short inquiry as part of a unit on plants or a yearlong focus that integrates a number of scientific concepts (as well as literacy, math, and social skills). Tree data can be shared online ("my tree, your tree") and used as evidence of green space or global warming. An in-depth study of any phenomenon allows the student to consider it in a number of different ways. While one teacher might want to "explore nature," another might want students to examine whether all people have access to these natural spaces. In the next section, I consider some aspects of local studies in relation to three specific subjects.

Social Studies Investigations

Jeff Hindes, a middle school social studies teacher who uses the term "setting" for the "narration of history," believes when students are able to picture the events in a familiar setting, it leads to a deeper understanding. As a teacher of history, he seeks "authentic discovery moments" that will serve as the foundation for future learning. "I'd say that it's my natural way of teaching in the sense that history for me has always been personal ... history's tangible," he says. His commitment to the rigors of the discipline propels him outside the school so students can engage in original inquiry. This kind of personal inspiration prompts him to seek out primary sources, field experiences, and local narratives that students can situate history in a place they know.

> *"For me history is tangible... . I like using the local hook to bring kids—to draw them in."*

Jeff believes that providing the local context gives students "touchstones" to process the information, "touchstones in the sense of keeping things real." His use of the word "touchstone" shows how multiple connections provide an experiential context and also serve as a centerpiece for a deeper subject study: "We can talk about it on a national scale and how these things were changing the nation, but all of that stuff is here, and so it becomes something they pass every day or something that they can go visit or just [have] an image in their mind."

While studying the Civil War, Jeff uses the essential question, "How did the Civil War affect Vermonters?" (the state where he teaches). He asks students to delve into local sources and field experiences alongside the examination of the national narrative. By investigating journals, photos, maps, letters from soldiers, and a visit to an Underground Railroad site, he believes students gained a deeper understanding of US history as well as an ability to analyze the local implications of a national event. He describes how "we talk about these things in the greater scheme of things and then bring them local." His unit has traditional topics such as soldier life, the Emancipation Proclamation, the role of African Americans, and women, but throughout the unit, he maintains a local narrative to build students' ability to answer the essential question and better understand the Civil War.

Language Arts Investigations

English teachers understand the power of authentic questions. When finding ways to engage students in the large questions of human existence, a high school English teacher begins by thinking about her students:

> So much of literature is based on the large human questions. This is what I want my students to grapple with: literature that relates to their own experience as human beings and understandings that will accompany them through their lives. English class is about life.

Another high school English teacher with a similar view uses the local context to explore the visions of utopia suggested in literature. He challenged his high school students to envision a future society while reading books such as *1984, Summerhill, Ecotopia,* and *Brave New World* and to apply them to their own communities. Students were challenged to imagine their own futures in ways that might "move them forward to a more meaningful life." By asking students to use a local setting, their imagination could gain more traction. Students asked what utopia might actually look like in the places where they lived.

Setting is one of those big ideas in language arts that is often taught with no attention to how students perceive their own surroundings. A librarian wanted her students to write stories set in their hometown, so she organized a bus tour so students could visit different possible "settings." On the tour, they considered story possibilities and had the chance to record details they would use in their writing. Like good writers, they did the research.

Hero is another concept that can be more actively contextualized; it has so much to do with what young people aspire to. A pre-service language arts teacher designed a unit for middle-level students to study the concept of hero and think about the heroes in their local community. The plan was to examine how people view heroes while reading a variety of genres. They would consider traditional literary topics such as the traits of a hero, their powers and flaws, and how history views heroes. She asks students to consider: "In what ways am I a hero?" and "Who are the heroes in our community?" The language she uses to assess their work reflects this dual purpose. She asks that they *"analyze methods used to portray heroic traits in myths, comics, the media and in news articles"* alongside the task to *"identify heroic traits in self and community members."* In a "regular" lesson plan, she asks them to identify heroic traits and asks who in the community exhibits these traits. They complete a persona inventory, discuss heroes in the community, and make a plan to interview a community hero.

Investigating the concept of "hero" can lead to interesting conversations about who students look up to and why. Some musicians, athletes, and others take on the status of "hero" in ways that we might want young learners to examine more closely. For example, students in California took part in a Media Arts and Humanities "Resilience Café Project" (Kerr & Staff, 2011) in which they connected a historical figure, a community member whom they respected, and their own personal story of resilience. Through writing and artistic expression, they represented and shared their new learning with community members in an evening of music, spoken word, and artistic expression.

Science Investigations

Science journals are a perfect tool for local studies. Whatever big concept is under study, students can keep a journal asking the question, What is happening here? Springtime is a lovely time to do this and can be done in conjunction with a weather unit, a unit on birds, migration, plants, or climate change. Some science journals are very informal; others can be highly technical. Journals employ writing, thinking, observation, and delving into scientific phenomenon the way real scientists do.

A critical view of teaching science would be to shift the questions from the science content to the social context in which knowledge may be put to use. While this is the focus of Chapter 6, it is important to consider alongside subjects to illustrate the rigor present in such a shift. Buxton (2010) conducted a study of middle-level students learning about environmental issues and the implications for human health. Students analyzed the safety of tap water and "designer" bottled water within a larger discussion of access to healthy water worldwide ("my water, your water, all water"). Buxton contrasts this approach to "decontextualized" science and concludes that "students who are meaningfully engaged in social problem solving can still learn the science they need to pass state assessments while focusing on the value of science as a tool for promoting social justice" (p. 122).

The call to authentically "do the science" is enriched by the many opportunities presented by the Internet that share findings and data for different purposes. For example, the Cornell Lab of Ornithology (www.birds.cornell.edu//citsci/projects) has a number of "citizen science" resources. One of the links, "Celebrate Urban Birds" (http://celebrateurbanbirds.org), holds a challenge called "Fascinating Feathers" to share photos, video, poetry, stories, or audio in the following fun categories: best camouflage, best dressed, most bizarre, and most functional.

Bio-Mimicry (http://ben.biomimicry.net) provides a provocative context for exploring design solutions and local inquiry. Bio-mimicry poses that we can learn how to solve problems if we pay attention to how nature has engineered, evolved, and designed solutions to the benefit of different species. It integrates a number of scientific principles and provides stunning examples of what we can see if we look closely ... at the movement of a snail, the design of a feather, or at an insect with "living mechanical gear." Such an insect was discovered by scientists who found that, in order to jump, its body parts intermeshed like a regular gear (Hooker, 2013). The wonder of what we can discover on the Internet is more significant when students can find real-world verification of amazing happenings.

Students find it thrilling to share new information, more so when using 21st-century technologies. An eighth-grade student of Barry Guillot (see p. 77) expresses enthusiasm for teaching younger students about swamp critters: "I presented the alligator to over 50,000 people last year, but showing them to the third-graders on the webcam Skyping was a much different experience! It was so cool to see their excitement and hear their excitement through the computer!"

What Is a River?

Rivers can be a site to understand many scientific principles such as erosion, gravity, hydrology, geology, and velocity. A "River Unit" could very easily be focused on just science and be structured to learn about one ecosystem, or a way to understand hydrology or aquatic food webs. If you wanted students to have better understanding of rivers globally, they could study many aspects of rivers worldwide—including one nearby. This unit ("What Is a River?"; see Figure 4.2) reflects a way to better understand rivers around the world through looking at a nearby river and consider ways that people experience rivers in different places and in different ways. The variety of perspectives invites a multidisciplinary study, and the purpose of the unit remains to understand rivers through a subject-based or multi-subject lens. Rivers enhance the understanding of science, mathematics, social studies, language arts, and the arts. It remains a subject-based study because the subjects remain identifiable. The focus here is not "my river" or a particular river's influence on one place but to deepen understanding of all rivers and the systems and principles that govern them.

★★★★★★★★★★

When it becomes more about understanding the river nearby—then it becomes more about place and "my river" than about all rivers. The next approach described in Chapter 5 reflects the ways that real places invite a multidisciplinary or an interdisciplinary study, and the purpose shifts from the mastery of subjects to a more holistic understanding of a local place. Deep, authentic subject-based investigations of nearby places (as described here in Chapter 4) most often—given space and time—lead to the more integrated stories of our places (Chapter 5).

★★★★★★★★★★

ESSENTIAL QUESTION: WHAT IS A RIVER?

Introductory Lesson #1: What is a river? What does it mean to me?

To begin, explore the essential questions with students' memories and experiences with a local river. Begin a nature/human interaction observation journal. Ask how this river compares to other rivers in the world. Explore the many ways that humans interact with "our river" and how that relationship has changed over time.

Formative Lesson Ideas:

Rivers around the World: What do rivers mean to people around the world? What are the different ways that people and rivers interact? OUTCOME: Identify initial categories: commerce, travel, pleasure, energy, etc.

World Rivers: What role have rivers played in human history? OUTCOME: Illustrated Timeline of Human Activity and World Rivers.

Human Impact: How do people value, use, harm, and celebrate rivers around the world? How do we treat our river? OUTCOME: Portrait of a Riverkeeper (local or global).

Our River—Stories over Time: Ethnographic research of community members and their relationship with a local river. OUTCOME: Vignette: A Time in History that portrays how humans interact with a river.

Rich Text and the River of Love: How writers and artists communicate their feelings about rivers. Read anthology of global river writing. Invite local artists to exhibit their work in school. Individual inquiry about other artistic expressions around the world. OUTCOME: Personal/Artistic Expression of "What is a river?"

Exemplary River Research: Case Study: Learning about a River: Explore one river as a whole class to present exemplary research practice as model for group projects. OUTCOME: Model of River Research Final Project. Consider what makes an excellent research project.

Begin River Research: Groups of students will focus on one river and explore the different questions set forth in Lessons 1–6. OUTCOME: Criteria for Research Project developed with class.

River Keepers: Guest Presentation by Local Citizen/Stewardship Group: How do people take care of their rivers and waterways? OUTCOME: Begin to define what a community plan for celebrating the local river might look like. Include in plan reference to similar efforts in other parts of the world.

Nature Journal of River Spot: Compiled throughout unit. OUTCOME: Each student contributes a page that combines a local and global expression of "what is a river?" to class digital "River Book."

Planning for the Culminating Activity: Research Learning Circles: Students Share Research in near Final Drafts. Critique and Revision. Jigsaw discussion on how to host Public Event to share Findings and stimulate community involvement in river.

CULMINATING ACTIVITY: Summative Assessment to Essential Question

EVENT: Students share research, "River Book," and community portraits in public event. Students host dialogue in which community responds to the questions: What is a River? What does it mean to us? In what ways might our actions preserve and celebrate this river?

RESEARCH SUMMARY: Students record, compile, interpret, and present a plan for community participation. OUTCOME: Community Action Plan.

PERSONAL RESPONSE: Student Reflection: Written piece on "What is a River?" "What does it mean to me?"

FIGURE 4.2

Amy B. Demarest, Place-based Curriculum Design: Exceeding Standards through Local Investigations. © Routledge, 2015.

References

Buxton, C. A. (2010). Social problem solving through science: An approach to critical, place-based, science teaching and learning. *Equity & Excellence in Education, (43)*1, 120–135. http://dx.doi.org/10.1080/10665680903408932

Colchester High School. (2012). Colchester in a time of globalization [Unpublished classroom document]. Colchester, VT: Rachel Wood's Geography classroom.

Cribbs, S., Newman, B., & Even, N. (2009). Outside the lens. *Unboxed, 3*, 30–37.

Hooker, G. (2013, September 17). Living mechanical gear [Web log message]. Retrieved December 5, 2013, from http://ben.biomimicry.net/coolbio/2013/living-mechanical-gear/

Jenson-Elliott, C. (2011). Canyon as classroom. *Unboxed, (4)*2, 6–15.

Kerr, I., & Staff, C. (2011). Resilience Café Project cards. *Unboxed,* 7. Retrieved November 12, 2013, from http://hightechhigh.org/unboxed/issue7/cards/4.php

Kriesberg, D. (2000). A reverence for place. *Connect, 14*(1), 5–8.

Shelton, J. (2006). Alabama silos: A conversation with Jack Shelton. *Democracy and Education, 16*(2), 6–9.

Smith, G. (2007, March). *Keynote.* The 4th Promise of Place Conference, Fairlee, VT.

Toolin, R., & Watson, A. (2010). Students for sustainable energy: Inspiring students to tackle energy projects in their school and community. *Science Teacher,* 77(4), 27–31.

Wood, R. (2012). Colchester in a time of globalization: A photo essay project assignment [Unpublished classroom document]. Colchester, VT: Rachel Wood's Geography classroom.

TEACHER PORTRAIT #4
ELLEN TEMPLE
MIDDLE

"I want them to have their own words for the local pond."

Ellen came to place-based education through her own deep connection to the power of writing. She is herself a writer, received her master's from the Bread Loaf School of English, and is on the Leadership Council of National Writing Project in Vermont. As a teacher of writing, it has always been about students making connections to what is around them. Knowing that good writers write about what they know, it just makes sense to her to "write what's close." She believes that students' writing improves when they have real reasons to write and a real audience for their work.

The writing projects that she asks her students to undertake are imaginative and rigorous; they head out to the nearby village to witness moments of everyday life and learn to listen intently when people talk. In a "reporter-at-large" assignment, they identify a place in town to conduct an interview about a chosen topic. "The idea is to get inside a place and capture its essence, the feel of the place," says Ellen.

The sensory monologue is about learning to really observe. "They go somewhere and sit for 15 minutes, which is a long time for fifth-graders, and just take notes. The next day they [...] rewrite it into something meaningful. The directions are pretty vague on purpose. A lot of them become poems ... almost spontaneously. Some of them become letters to people. One boy wrote to his cousin who had spent the summer in Vermont. They had hung out at a [certain] place and he wrote about going back there."

They write and perform one- to two-minute conversations that students reproduce or invent but that are rooted in their experience. For weeks, they write and then they perform monologues that "capture their lives, on the playground, at the dinner table; it's about them." Ellen often stages authentic recitations and sees a final performance of a writing piece as "giving back." "We focus on whether the language is right for the situation ... Because they share it, it gets more precise. [...] And they always want to do more. They want more. It's about them."

Ellen also team-teaches social studies. As part of a local geography lesson, she assigns a mapping activity for students to assimilate different sources in an initial attempt to locate their watershed. Small groups work with four different maps to figure out where their houses are in relation to the town's main tributary. Some students struggled. Others eagerly worked through the task exclaiming: "Oh I know where that river ends up" or "I can tell which road is marked here." She ponders the complexity of the task when they are challenged to resolve the maps with what they already know: "They have to think more ... they do have to work harder at making sense of it. I can't hand it to them on a little silver platter like I could a worksheet."

On her desk is a sign that says: "Being told is the opposite of finding out." When I asked her about it she responded: "I think that's how I teach as much as possible."

5

LOCAL INVESTIGATIONS BUILD HOLISTIC UNDERSTANDING OF PLACES

"A particular place on earth can be a kind of curricular lens through which all traditional subjects may be closely examined."

Paul Theobold & John Siskar (2008, p. 216)

LOCAL INVESTIGATIONS BUILD HOLISTIC UNDERSTANDING OF PLACES	
How can I help students better understand this place?	
Social Studies Science Mathematics PLACE Art Language Arts	Teachers pose questions about local places as organizing themes for students to learn about the places where they live. The character, history, details, and needs of a place emerge as students explore the "stories of places" through a multidisciplinary or an interdisciplinary lens. The stories they uncover may combine subjects in different ways that reflect the complexity of places, but the emphasis remains on understanding the place.

FIGURE 5.1

Amy B. Demarest, Place-based Curriculum Design: Exceeding Standards through Local Investigations. © Routledge, 2015.

In the third element, a place serves as a unifying construct for a multidisciplinary or an interdisciplinary study. Teachers plan learning based on questions that arise from places. Place-based questions are broader than subject-based studies and always encompass more than one discipline. There is more of a focus on learning about the place than learning the subject, although subject mastery remains a key undertaking. The distinction between this approach and the element outlined in Chapter 4 is that here the emphasis is on the place, whatever the story. When the story of a place emerges, subjects can merge beyond recognition. This chapter presents how a place can serve as an organizing construct for curriculum and, within that construct, offer a span of multi- and interdisciplinary learning opportunities.

"Beyond the science of a place—a more integrated, greater brush stroke across a place."

Exploring the different stories of a place invites answers from many disciplines. In an interdisciplinary or a multidisciplinary approach, the place serves as an integrating construct for an academic study. The weight of the endeavor shifts from the subject to the place and the story it tells. Subject mastery is built as students seek a holistic understanding about their local environment. To learn about the local place, you might dig into the history story, the ecology story, or the geology story; you might write poems, collect data, and interview the residents. The learning goes where the place leads. Standards come together.

Subjects Merge in Place-based Studies

If you studied food in the context of one place, you would find many interesting questions. In California, teachers used a prominent characteristic of the place they lived—the work of the migrant workers in nearby strawberry fields—to begin to examine their community (Saifer, Edwards, Ellis, Ko, & Stuczynski, 2011). They asked students to graph the number of years that people had worked in the fields. The focus was on an important aspect of a place; it provided an engaging context on how to make a graph and led students to learn much more about the farmers and their place. If another teacher asked students to learn about where their food comes from, they might examine transportation, local stores, buying habits, and the work farmers do to get a clearer picture of a local food system. They might learn about land use, farming, agricultural history, recipes, and culturally based eating traditions, but all those would be explored to understand food in one place.

When students discover authentic questions in their communities, the pursuit of an answer often does not stay within designated subjects. A group of sixth-graders who tackled the problem of emissions from buses idling outside their school demonstrated this to their teacher who wrote in a reflective journal:

> As the students' projects unfolded . . . they started learning so many things we hadn't anticipated . . . without our having planned it, they were interviewing, sorting and presenting data, writing persuasively, calculating challenging math problems, working collaboratively, and speaking publicly. These were not outcomes that we had planned—but emerged in their work.

A teacher may start with what she thinks is a single subject study and quickly find out that the work crosses subject boundaries. Perhaps a teacher begins by looking at a parcel of land through an ecological lens but realizes students need to understand the history of land use to fully comprehend the problem. Or a student needs math to solve a problem or interpret a phenomenon. Students go outside to write poetry, but they find an interesting bug they want to learn more about. If students are looking closely at a place, there is no guarantee that their findings will remain a "social studies problem" or a "science problem." Matt Dubel (2006) describes this in relation to a geology study in which he took part:

> As a science exploration, we began to explore the basic geology, but the human connection to the rock was so persuasive that we were propelled into social studies. The social studies investigation yielded data that told the story quantitatively, so we launched into mathematics. And communicating what we discovered to a broader audience necessitated language arts. To leave out any discipline not only would have weakened the academic rigor of the project, it would have foreclosed that natural human curiosity to see where the story leads without regard to academic categories.
>
> *(pp. 7–8)*

I love the language of this description. The words used to describe this study— "propelled," "launched," and "necessitated"—portray an active view of curriculum. What began as a geology study was taken in different directions by the connections the students made. The story of the place directed the learning and redefined the outcome. In taking a study "where the story leads," as Dubel reflects, students' understanding is richer and grounded in the world they inhabit.

In this way, the essential question that emerges from a place may be a combination of standards (big ideas) from different subjects. Students might consider human impact (ecology), change over time (history), and stewardship (civics) in order to examine what have been the environmental changes over time and how people have dealt with them. If the question of economic livelihood and corporate responsibility were added into the mix, students could consider in what ways people have helped or hurt the environment and how these actions have affected peoples' lives.

MULTIDISCIPLINARY QUESTIONS THAT EMERGE FROM PLACES

What is the story of this place?
What is a community?
How has our neighborhood changed over time?
What is a watershed?
What is important for people to know about our town?
How do people in this place express themselves?
Is our neighborhood walkable?
How do we care for this land and water?
How has this river shaped our community?
Who lives in this city/neighborhood?

In an interdisciplinary study in which a place is the integrating concept, the subjects can remain recognizable. Teachers use places to "do" the history, math, science, and so forth. The content gets covered in the context of a local place. This can be very structured or highly fluid. When I taught about the Lake Champlain Basin (Demarest, 1997), I structured the delivery of subjects in tandem with scientific inquiry, engaging field experiences, interesting guest speakers, and authentic writing; however, the impetus for this learning was to learn about the Lake Champlain Basin. The place determined what we studied and shaped the subject emphasis. I had never taught geology but found it was central to the story, so I learned more about rocks than I ever might have imagined. Even though there were often unintended results, things kept pretty much to the plan that I designed. Students developed a sense of the "whole story" of this bioregion and could also tell you about its history, ecology, geography, and geology. More than once, an adult exclaimed: "Your students know more about the issues facing this lake than most of the adults who live here!"

Teachers Define Places Differently

When I began teaching in Vermont, political borders defined how I viewed "local." When I focused more on the Lake Champlain Basin instead of the state of Vermont, the natural boundaries of where water flowed defined the place we studied. Natural features or scientific concepts can define the parameters of place—such as an ecosystem, meadow, or quarry. Neighborhoods, cities, and regions all can establish a definition of place. Places are defined by political boundaries, natural boundaries, or individually determined boundaries. The concepts that help you define the place often reflect a standard (i.e., state or bioregion) that you are learning about in a certain time and place.

How a teacher defines the place will determine the nature of the investigation. Different places—rivers, neighborhoods, regions, city blocks, or schoolyards—pose different questions. Cindy Jenson-Elliott (2011) discovered a canyon in the backyard of the school where she was interviewing for a job—a job that she accepted the next day with the understanding that she could use the canyon as a learning site:

> Taking a walk around the neighborhood, I saw that in back of the park next to the school, the earth dropped away into a broad, sloping canyon, which ended in a busy street. It was an entrance to Tecolote Canyon—trashy, scraped bare and left for the colonization of weeds. But the slope had a few healthy stands of native plants—lemonadeberry, chamise, buckwheat and sagebrush—all evidence that underneath the thrashed veneer, a healthy ecosystem still struggled to exist. I walked farther into the neighborhood and found more canyon access points that led to trickling creeks, oak woodlands, and chaparral and coastal sage scrub ecosystems. All were within walking distance of the school.

(p. 8)

Jenson-Elliott defined the parameters of her study from the natural boundaries of the canyon. She continues: "For my science students, grades 1–8, using a specific natural place in our community—Tecolote Canyon—as both a subject and place of study could provide us with an ever-changing, living textbook from which to learn basic ecological concepts and develop a relationship with the natural world" (p. 9).

If studying the Great Plains, issues of agriculture, native traditions, and water and land use would be critical. If studying a city block, questions might emerge about community, history, food equity, or fair housing. Water sources and ecosystems can be explored in urban settings, as well as traffic patterns and issues of development in rural places. In the Southwest, it would be hard to study the history of a town without raising questions about water sources. In the South, it would be hard to study agriculture without learning about slavery. When asking local questions, it is harder to deny the interconnecting parts of the whole story.

Amy LaChance's second- and third-grade students at the Sustainability Academy at Lawrence Barnes (2013) in Burlington worked on a book titled *A Walk Down North Street*. They used old and current photographs and researched many of the buildings on this street that runs the length of one of our oldest and most culturally diverse neighborhoods. The students learned that there were waves of immigrants that came here over a long time and that the buildings told many of the stories of this community. One group of students wrote about the Himalayan Market:

Our building is 97 North Street. It was built between 1889–1894. In 1900 it was a creamery. In the apartment upstairs lived a shoemaker. This small two-story building is home to the Himalayan Market and an apartment. It is a store that sells rice, goat, and beans for example. If you want something from Nepal, head over!

(p. 24)

A student's drawing of the market:

Dylan Grimm. Used with permission.

At City High School in Tucson, Arizona (http://cityhighschool.org), the theme for ninth grade is "Tucson as Textbook." Students explore the different parts of the city and the environment, interview residents, and find time to celebrate their heritage and community. Much of their work focuses on a "neighborhood study" that breaks the city into sections. Students seek out the story of one section of their city. That is the place that they have defined.

At the end of the year, the same students were asked to consider the changes that might come to their city in the future. Students researched buildings and worked with a local architect and other community members to envision urban transformations. One student who learned the history of an old theater imagined it coming to life in 20 years when City High School students (still doing the same urban investigations) met up with the great-great granddaughter of the original owner. The student's "vision" was of how the descendant refurbished the theater with the help of her architect husband:

> . . . leaving lots of its original historical character throughout. He created a metal shade structure to prevent the building from overheating in the hot Arizona sun, and Carmen planted flowering vines to offer more shade. They converted the roof into a hangout place, with chic couches and fire and glass features. Though the outside is a bumping, hip and sleek place at night, the inside remains a cozy Mexican bakery full of family history, which is displayed in historic photos throughout the interior.
>
> *(City High School, 2010)*

After the students' writing and artwork was compiled and mapped into a guide, Tucson residents were invited on a bike tour of the buildings where they could stop and examine the present and future possibilities of certain buildings in the downtown.

A student's rendition of the Teatro Carmen:

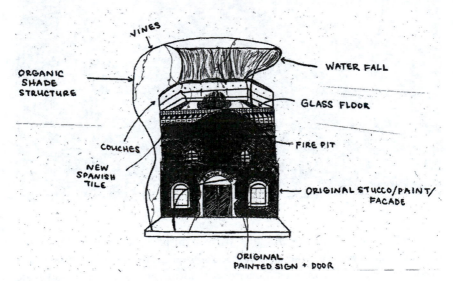

City High School. Used with permission.

What Is the Story of This Place?

Delving into the nature of places requires a wider lens and a more complex structure than a subject-based study. While you might get a solid understanding of a river by studying river ecology, you cannot get the feel of a town by just studying its history or science. You cannot explore the "soul" of a city block without being open to a wide array of questions. Multi- and interdisciplinary studies strive toward a holistic understanding of a place rather than knowledge broken into disparate parts. John Elder (1998) uses the analogy of an ecotone where different habitats merge to express the richness of a study that combines multiple disciplines. Such studies, he believes, benefit our students and the well-being of the places we learn about. Students can explore provocative questions emanating from a place, not through a specific subject lens but from what places conjure up. Elder (1998) believes that subject-based lenses shunt our ability to personally discover the richness and wonders of the places we live:

> We wonder at the world's amazing variety, we love it for its beauty. These truths are at the heart of attentiveness to nature, and we educators need to assert them with some defiance in the face of disciplines that pride themselves on their presumptive objectivity.
>
> *(p. 10)*

Elementary teachers manage organizing the melding of subjects the easiest. A K–1 teacher organized a medley of wonderful investigations of her neighborhood based on the essential question, *What is the story of this place?* Her kindergarten students explored buildings, ferns, legends, town leaders, and roads all to better understand and ask questions about the place where they lived—as six- and seven-year-olds. They were able to get outside to investigate, and the classroom was rich with storybooks, relics, pictures, and experiments related to the local stories they were tracking down.

In middle school, grade-level teams of teachers often approach the study of place with a multidisciplinary or an interdisciplinary approach. A team might undertake the study of their town, and each teacher might organize their subject and address content standards using a geographical place as an "organizing center" (Beane, 1997). While there would still be recognizable subject mastery, the nature of a place will illuminate the connections between disciplines.

Barry Guillot, a middle school science teacher who teaches near Lake Pontchartrain near New Orleans (www.wetlandwatchers.org), has devoted, with his students, more than 10 years to "transform a fragile 28-acre former dump-site into a living wetlands classroom" (Kielsmeier, 2010, p. 10). Now a nationally known service-learning project, the work has expanded to incorporate art, technology, engineering, and math. Guillot began as a way for his students to "utilize our beautiful Louisiana wetlands as an outdoor classroom where students could be fully immersed in science while learning the many values of our wetlands and the many challenges they face" (personal communication, November 6, 2013).

"I think that the students we speak to want to be like us! We show them that they can also be a world-changer!"

Guillot shares that their work has generated 35 "solid partnerships"—all of whom appear to feel honored to work with the students. One of their partners, the Crescent Soil and Water Conservation District, acknowledges the real contributions the students make: "[It] makes our job, of promoting soil and water conservation in our community, a lot easier and a lot more effective." Another partner from the USDA comments:

> Being able to participate in the Wetland Watchers project is a wonderful experience for me. I enjoy speaking and showing the students the soils, plants, and other natural resources native to this area. I know that I am connecting with these students by the questions they ask and the interest they take in our demonstrations. From an agency perspective, we reach more people through these educational activities than any other program we conduct.
>
> *(Guillot, personal communication, November 6, 2013)*

This Louisiana swamp has become a place of learning. Not only do community experts work alongside students, but seventh-graders also serve as mentors to younger students and teach them about wetlands, what creatures live there, and how to collect data at the site. The students report that teaching the younger students is rewarding, that they love to "see their eyes light up" and share the excitement. "We show them that they can be a world-changer," says one student. Another student comments, "I think if the animals and plants could talk, they'd say that we're their heroes because that is the way I feel when I work in the Wetlands." It was the particular place, its characteristics and "needs," that determined the work that Guillot's students accomplished.

Barry Guillot. Used with permission.

In an interdisciplinary or a multidisciplinary study, the teacher has the opportunity to guide the student in integrating the "answer" in an authentic way. She, or a team of teachers, would still be able to track discipline-specific skills to include scientific understanding, writing and technology skills, or an ability to analyze text. A science teacher and a history teacher together might ask their students: "What would a viable land-use plan be for this tract of land?" A language arts teacher might partner with the town/city offices to improve signage in the community about the local "story." She could administer an assessment of language arts, but the information would have history and science information as well.

High schools face a larger challenge to meld subjects, but it is being done through block scheduling, team configurations, and a belief in how students learn best. The pull of subjects may be strongest at this level, but teachers are finding ways to make them more connected. Social studies and English teachers find ways to join together for a "humanities" approach to issues, and science-math-technology teachers join up for real-world problem solving. Alternative programs more easily make the leap to adjusting the whole of the school day toward authentic pursuits while still accommodating subject requirements.

Attention to science, technology, engineering, and mathematics (STEM) work is inviting more instances of integrated work in the high schools when integration of STEM is the implicit challenge. A group of teachers can work together to facilitate an investigation into alternative energy practices. The science class can research alternative energy—the math teacher can analyze data and track usage patterns. The social studies teacher can map and analyze patterns of energy use, and the language arts teacher can organize interviews that reveal people's changing habits and attitudes.

Gay describes how their high school study of Lewis Creek study is organized:

> When everybody's on board, we go to the river and have five stations. The health teacher was working with students to design personal fitness plans, so they went on a hike and figured out heart rate, etc. In science, we conducted the chemical and biological tests. The math teacher had them do a floating experiment she designed to determine velocity and total discharge. The history teacher explored land use change around Lewis Creek from the 1600s to the present. With the English teacher, students created an art/poetry piece with nature writing and journaling.

Brett Goble, a humanities teacher at City High School (2012) merged family history with literacy skills when his students researched the stories behind their family recipes. They wrote a book titled *American Studies Family Recipe Book*. This student writes about her family's allegiance to chocolate chip cookies:

THE FAMILY OF CHOCOLATE CHIP COOKIES BY SIERRA LINDSAY

My family doesn't tell stories. The only ones I can remember are short, funny quips from vacations before I was born, where bobcats peeked over old Native American ruins and lightening [sic] storms washed my parents out of a picnic on Mt. Lemmon. Our ancestors were not relatives of Laura Ingalls Wilder, nor were they of high political stature and did not leave some grand legacy behind. There are no stories. I guess that means we are the story.

My family is a congregation of sarcastic, large-lunged, long-winded people. We laugh too long and talk too loud. We ask too much and give too little. That is a story if you have heard one, right?

Sometimes I find it hard to be a part of my family. . . . Sometimes it's hard to see eye to eye with all the opinionated, very outspoken individuals that make up the Lindsay clan. But more often than not, I am grateful.

Though we may not have many stories, I have one that I've decided to tell. Have you ever stood in front of a lit oven, staring through the glass at a batch of slowly rising chocolate chip cookies? I have. Have you ever licked the batter off a mixer's appendage, cleaning every edge shiny with your tongue? I have. This is a constant of my childhood, the scent of warm cookies, the scatter of chocolate chips on the counter as they leap for the bowl, the whir and scrape of the mixer as it throws spots of dough everywhere it can. All of the segments and groups of our family have a dish, some food that represents them. For a time, we were the family of chocolate chip cookies.

Our cookies were a Christmas tradition, I was puffed up like a turkey every Christmas Eve, smug beyond compare that Santa was going to get the privilege of tasting our prided cookies. And every morning, when only crumbs of them remained. I would strut about the house with my presents, knowing that Santa had surely never tasted better.

We don't tell stories. We have our words and our actions, our living and dying. We are not a family of stories, but we are the family of chocolate chip cookies. And if that isn't a story, then what is? (p. 13)

Treasures as Stories

A teacher can use a broad concept like treasures to find the stories of a place. She might frame a short lesson, an inquiry, or an entire unit on the idea of the treasures that places hold. Instead of thinking of treasures as related to specific subjects, she may want her students to define "treasures" (see Lesson One in Figure 5.2). An essential question such as "What are our local treasures?" poses a different inquiry

> ## ESSENTIAL QUESTION: WHAT ARE OUR LOCAL TREASURES?
>
> ### Introductory Lesson #1: What are treasures? How might we define treasures?
>
> Explore personal and collective views of people and places as community treasures. Share poetry, songs, and writings that explore the concept of treasures. Ask students to bring in an artifact or image that represents a personal treasure. Discuss the associations these treasures have with specific places and create an initial "treasure map" of the community.
>
> ### Formative Lesson Ideas:
>
> ***What are treasures? How might we define treasures?*** Explore students' special places. Make a treasure map of students' special places.
>
> ***What are the different treasures our community values?*** Interview parents and neighbors about what is special to them in their community. Create initial definition of what a community treasure is. Discuss a research plan for searching out and documenting treasures.
>
> ***Who are our treasures?*** Meet a treasure: Invite a town elder to come and visit and share his or her view of history and what is important to living well. Ask students to artistically represent these living treasures.
>
> ***Where are our treasures?*** Visit a treasure. Visit a local "special place" on a field trip and investigate it through a variety of lenses. Discover its historical, ecological, aesthetic, and fun "stories." When you return to class, ask students to represent why they think this place is a treasure.
>
> ***Are all treasures really treasures? Is our definition of treasures inclusive and respectful to all?*** Students examine a museum that houses some "treasures" with different interpretations and explore different viewpoints.
>
> ***What is happening in our community to help protect our treasures? What threatens our treasures?*** Share community activist presentation of threatened green space as an example.
>
> ***What treasures are important to preserve? Are there treasures in our community that are threatened in some way?*** Invite a guest speaker from a group that is working to preserve ethnic heritage/cultural heritage. Is this something that we want to and can do something about? Explore possible class service project.
>
> ***What do I want to know about our community treasures?*** Research Project: Students work in groups to define, document, and preserve a community treasure. Students become experts on a particular kind of treasure (i.e., "peaceful places expert," "natural places expert," "threatened places expert," "safe places expert").
>
> ### CULMINATING ACTIVITY: Summative Assessment to Essential Question
>
> PRODUCT will include:
>
> - Individual Portfolio of Community Map of Treasures as defined by class and student,
> - Group Presentation of Research on Local Treasures,
> - Service Component that educates audience about community treasures, and
> - Personal Reflection on Essential Question: What are our local treasures? How are they important to me?

FIGURE 5.2

Amy B. Demarest, Place-based Curriculum Design: Exceeding Standards through Local Investigations. © Routledge, 2015.

than the question, "What is the history of our place?" To investigate treasures, the class would have to explore the concept of "treasures" and experience some local examples of how treasures are viewed. They may find some hidden treasures and bring them forth to consider in new and unexpected ways, using the skills and dispositions of many disciplines.

Since the word *treasures* suggests personal values, it is an opportunity for students to explore their own values as well as what members of their community "treasure." A museum might house a historic relic such as a Confederate flag, an auction block, or a Native American weaving. How do different individuals view these artifacts? Decisions made by museums or "keepers of the treasures" might be challenged and amended as students examine different perspectives in regard to a community's material culture.

This overview of a unit based on the question, *What are our local treasures?* is a plan for students to uncover the treasures of their community. The authentic, nearby application of subjects is used to suggest different perspectives on the meaning of "treasure," but the final understanding is about the place. It is a plan that can be used in any place.

★★★★★★★★★★

As exemplified by the treasures unit, an interdiscplinary or a multidisciplinary study can be organized so the culminating activity is a chance for the student to make complex connections. The "answer" that emerges from a place might be more relevant than a single-subject "answer." Rather than the teacher directing a summary in the different subjects, students are asked to express their understanding in a holistic response. A teacher might build a unit on the essential question, *"What is important for your neighbors to know about this town?"* A certain level of subject mastery would be required. Her students could construct their own answers to the question and give a public presentation. Or a class might explore a unit on the question, *What is the future of our neighborhood?* Students would be required to demonstrate specific skills in mapmaking, writing, ethnography, technology, artistic representation, and oral communication. The final "answer" is designed by the student. To a large extent, the differences between this approach and the next rest in the extent to which the student articulates the outcome. It depends on what questions are asked and how students pursue answers.

★★★★★★★★★★

References

Beane, J. (1997). *Curriculum integration: Designing the core of democratic education.* New York, NY: Teachers College Press.

City High School. (2010). A tour of the future of downtown Tucson, Arizona. Tucson, AZ: Southwest Neighborhoods and Automobiles Association in conjunction with the Committee for the Future.

City High School. (2012). American studies family recipe book [Self-published classroom document]. Tucson, AZ: Brent Goble's American Studies classroom.

Demarest, A. (1997). *This lake alive! An interdisciplinary handbook for teaching and learning about the Lake Champlain Basin.* Shelburne, VT: Shelburne Farms.

Dubel, M. (2006). Of place and education: One intern's story. *Community Works Journal, 7*(3), 7–8, 33, 36.

Elder, J. (1998). Teaching at the edge. In J. Elder (Ed.), *Stories in the land: A place-based environmental education anthology* (pp. 1–13). In *Nature Literacy Series.* Great Barrington, MA: The Orion Society.

Jenson-Elliott, C. (2011). Canyon as classroom. *Unboxed, (4)*2, 6–15.

Kielsmeier, J. C. (2010). Build a bridge between service and learning. *Phi Delta Kappan*, *91*(5), 8–15.

Saifer, S., Edwards, K., Ellis, D., Ko, L., & Stuczynski, A. (2011). *Culturally responsive standards-based teaching: Classroom to community and back* (2nd ed.). A joint publication by Portland, OR: Education Northwest and Thousand Oaks, CA: Corwin Press.

Sustainability Academy at Lawrence Barnes. (2013). A walk down North Street looking at North Street's past, present and future: A journey through the Old North End of Burlington, Vermont [Self-published classroom document, with a grant from The Susan Sebastian Foundation]. Burlington, VT: Amy LaChance's multiage classroom.

Theobald, P., & Siskar, J. (2008). Place: Where diversity and community can converge. In D. Gruenewald & G. Smith (Eds.), *Place-based education in the global age: Local diversity* (pp. 197–219). Hillsdale, NJ: Lawrence Erlbaum Associates, Taylor and Francis Group.

TEACHER PORTRAIT #5
JEAN BERTHIAUME
HIGH SCHOOL

"We learn in the context of community."

Questions form the heart of Jean's curriculum. "It is always about the questions," he reflects. Jean believes that the most important questions come from students' own experiences. His classroom is a safe space where adolescents ponder the larger questions of selfhood and society. During a discussion of what teens had to deal with, one student told a story of how violence erupted in his home and he and his mother had to leave in the middle of the night with only a paper bag of clothes. After the student spoke, Jean said, "I think highly of you for sharing that personal story—I really appreciate it and want to recognize that." "Thanks," replied the student.

In another discussion, students were talking about cliques and students' attitudes toward each other. One student said, "They think I am trailer trash." Others shared their experiences of discrimination from their peers. Jean asked if there was anything that could be done. What started as one discussion, after much planning, collaboration, and hard work, ended as exquisite framed portraits hanging in the main hallway. Each included a written piece and a photograph of the author, professionally presented with help from students who had expertise in design and photography.

In his American History class, students made a film that was shown to the community. Townspeople gathered for the "World Premiere," the billing typical of both Jean's sense of celebration and the respect he gives student work. In this huge undertaking, students researched the time period of World War II to the present, interviewing local residents, and were tasked with presenting the local story within the context of the national narrative. The students were immensely proud of the final product and said the biggest challenge was to make the film a cohesive whole; they had to "figure out a lot of history and a lot of details." The audience was visibly moved. One parent said her son had not known his grandfather—who had died before he was born—"but he has come to know him through this film. I want to thank you."

Jean invites students to ponder inclusion, diversity, and acceptance in their own lives and mixes in issues of global importance. In the nationally recognized "Creating Sustainable Communities" curriculum, he asks students to consider their "sphere of influence." Students examine the global implications of their local actions and ask, "What are the things that we can do something about?"

Jean's ability to listen to, question, and challenge students is exquisite. He asks, If we're not talking about what's controversial, then what are we teaching? and believes that grappling with challenging issues provides the best opportunity for learning. He melds the personal, social, and intellectual nature of school and asks the same of his students. He spoke of how his identity as a gay man somehow freed him to be himself with his students: "I made a decision when I first went into teaching that I was going to be myself, and that opened up a door for me." Jean's pedagogy invites a similar honesty from his students and creates a safe, empowering place to learn.

6

LOCAL INVESTIGATIONS BUILD OPPORTUNITY FOR CIVIC ENGAGEMENT

"Creating a curriculum for and with young people begins with an examination of the problems, issues and concerns of life as it is being lived in the real world."

James Beane (1997, p. 40)

LOCAL INVESTIGATIONS BUILD OPPORTUNITY FOR CIVIC ENGAGEMENT	
How can I help students better understand themselves and their possible futures?	
	The teacher creates space for the student—in partnership with community members—to generate, explore, and address problems and issues that plague society. Subjects are mastered in the contexts of work done pursuing answers to students' questions. The teacher has not mapped out the direction or outcome of these inquiries; rather, they emerge from the work students do. This work alters traditional views of schoolwork and offers the student a new level of engagement and possibility.

FIGURE 6.1

Amy B. Demarest, Place-based Curriculum Design: Exceeding Standards through Local Investigations. © Routledge, 2015.

In the fourth aspect of this practice, students pursue authentic questions that emerge from the places where they live. Rather than topics embedded in traditional school subjects, this element is authentically linked to existing problems, dilemmas, and perplexities in the community. This approach reflects the "critical edge" of local inquiry that propels learning into new areas not always considered part of "regular" school. In addressing the questions that emerge from places, students have the opportunity to grapple with the real issues that impact their lives and their future. The work generated in this approach is linked to authentic needs in the community and the partnerships that form. It is in the doing, not just the study of it. The outcome is deep learning and real solutions. This chapter explores this more transformative approach to local inquiry when the student directs the investigation.

From a curricular view, this approach presents the learner as the designer of the investigation. Themes based on students' questions transcend subject boundaries. While all local investigations involve the self-direction of the student to a certain degree, this element alters the traditional structure of curriculum. If students investigate the need for economic revitalization in their community or issues that emerge from an ethnographic study or topics such as land use, stewardship, sustainable development, and systems, these ideas call for new frames that reorder subjects in a larger purpose. Grappling with these topics is new territory for the teacher that alters the topics, process, and outcomes of the work. Standards are still addressed, but it is a different planning process and often involves "back-mapping"— that is, the teacher will document particular learning goals after or alongside the tasks that are defined in collaboration with students and community members.

The Power of Integrated Curriculum

A teacher might want her students to explore the concept of healthy food for themselves, how it is viewed in the community, and whether there are service opportunities that would result from these investigations. A teacher might use the idea of "food deserts" (a provocative term that describes the lack of healthy food in some urban neighborhoods) to help her students explore the equity of food systems. As they learn about the benefits of healthy food, they might infer where they are in relation to these issues nationwide and address some questions to share with families. They might seek ways to make healthy food available and take this issue to the community. It might be structured in such a way to invite the larger questions. A teacher might say: "I was studying nutrition with my students and they became so intent on educating others that our learning became more about public service than healthy food."

When students investigate one aspect of a system, they invariably—given the nature of systems—are challenged to figure out other parts of the system. Students working on a school garden project will come into contact with local growers. They might end up learning about farmers' working conditions, soil health, pesticides, transportation, and the needs of their families. They start with one part of the problem but have to learn about the whole.

The larger "life" themes weave subjects together into essential questions that emerge from communities. The questions in this mode can be similar to those explored in the place-based approach (Part III); the difference depends on to what extent the teacher structures the pursuit of the answer in partnership with students. When in fourth grade, this student chose to take a picture of the playground and titled it "Recess Is Over."

Ian Drumm. Used with permission.

Educators often use the terms interdisciplinary, integrated, and integrative inter-changeably. James Beane (1997) points out a critical difference in these approaches in *Curriculum Integration: Designing the Core of Democratic Education*. He maintains that multi- or interdisciplinary studies are really not that different than single-subject studies, although they are often represented as models for integration. He discredits the continuums that present gradations of integration and suggests instead a separation between discipline-specific and integrated, period. "While there may be many shades and variations within them," he writes, "when it comes to the fate of the subject matter, there really are but two alternatives" (p. 13).

Beane's discussion of the role of students' questions is critical to understanding the power of this element of local investigations. He maintains that unless the structure emerges from the "social and personal concerns of students" (p. 15), the study is not truly integrative. It is in this sense that he views this approach as having the greatest potential for democracy—when students determine the path of their own learning. Kate reflects on this power: "You highlight democracy over and over when the teacher consults with the student about where they're going next. [It is sharing] the actual process of doing the planning and the learning."

Subject boundaries fade as students pursue authentic problems that encompass areas of the human experience beyond those outlined in a single or multiple disciplines. In what Beane terms "integrative curriculum," schoolwork emerges from authentic questions students have about their world. While these questions can address the knowledge of specific subjects, the goal is for students to seek and find a real "answer." While a teacher using this approach may still use the study of history or geography as a foundation for a larger inquiry, service, personal development, and community renewal may be activated in pursuit of the question.

"When you figure out what your questions are and where you are going to need to go to get the answers ... that is your curriculum."

A "bigger" purpose frames this work, and the student defines, and often structures, the task according the needs articulated by the group working on the problem. It is not just the subject outcome as defined by the teacher but the need for knowledge as determined by the student. The study may start with the questions from student concerns or an examination of a local problem, or it may be raised by an adult working with community concerns.

In this approach, there is still ample opportunity to learn and practice the standards, but they are tied to a higher purpose. The questions are different than a question posed within a particular subject or a gathering of subjects. Rather than ask, *"How has this community changed over time?"* (HISTORY), the question might be, *"How will this development affect different members of the community?"* Rather than ask, *"How does water testing indicate water health?"* (SCIENCE), the question might be, *"Does everyone have access to healthy water?"*

QUESTIONS ABOUT LIFE ADDRESSED IN LOCAL PLACES

What is the future of our neighborhood?
How do people in our town make decisions?
What is the quality of life in our town?
Why are kids in our school dropping out?
What will my future be?
Is my town safe?
Is our food healthy?
Where does our water come from and where does it go?
How are people in this place given help when they need it?
How do we treat each other?
What are the assets of this community?
In what way can I help make our neighborhood a better place to live?

Not all questions that students have about their world will be local questions. In fact, Beane's process of designing curriculum with students invites questions about self, community, and the world. After all three areas of questions are raised, teachers and students begin a process of curriculum mapping that weaves in all of these concerns. Lindsey Halman (see p. 61) uses this process with her middle school students to find the focus of their project-based learning time, which Halman runs as a parallel program alongside the "regular" curriculum. After looking at all their concerns, the students determined that "Technologically Advancing Technology" would be their theme for the year. They then spent time designing essential and focusing questions that defined their investigations and planned their inquiry.

Middle-schoolers at Birmingham Covington School in Bloomfield, Michigan, have tackled educating the local community about how sustainable their businesses are. They employ a number of discipline-related skills within the context of a bigger purpose. On their wiki, they write:

DOING BUSINESS IN BIRMINGHAM

We are fifth and sixth grade students at Birmingham Covington School and we have been learning about how local businesses fulfill the needs and wants of the local community. Birmingham is located in the heart of Oakland County and has a population of approximately twenty thousand. It is important to us that we live in a sustainable community. According to the United Nations Bruntland Report of 1987 "Sustainability is meeting the needs of the present without compromising the needs of future generations to meet their needs." This webpage is a resource for our local businesses to help them learn about the benefits of sustainability and the simple steps they can take to get there. We also have a honor roll page, which celebrates local businesses that are leading the way for Birmingham businesses to become sustainable. (Birmingham Covington School, 2013)
Read more at: http://doingbusinessinbirmingham.wikis.birmingham.k12. mi.us/#Vvw2g1gguYZaEb5e.99

Their teacher, Pauline Roberts (2013), describes the project in which she began with the questions that she then handed over to students to direct their investigations:

We began with two simple questions: What is the difference between a need and a want? and Who provides for our needs and wants in the community? We generated class definitions of needs and wants and began to look at various businesses and organizations that provided them. This led the students to consider sustainability: How are the businesses in our community ensuring that they are meeting the needs of the present while not compromising the needs of future generations?

In small groups of two or three, students began to organize their own information-gathering field trips, guided by their own areas of interests. With parent chaperones, our students visited hotels, hospitals, sports stadiums, theaters and museums in Detroit, armed with questionnaires and cameras to record their experiences. The level of engagement in this class skyrocketed, as students began to take charge of their own learning journeys. After every field trip students came back gushing about their research and what they had discovered. After analyzing their data [...] they decided to educate local business owners about sustainability and began to organize their learning into an informative WIKI that local business owners could refer to for tips and advice.

(p. 9)

Students made a brochure to share in the community that described their work and continued to gather information from local businesses. The site is a public service for the community. One of the things they created was an "Honor Roll" where they publicly post their findings. Students who worked on this project learned many things and reflected about the benefits of interacting with the community. Roberts shares (personal communication, October 23, 2013) her students' writings—one of whom reflected:

[One of the] most important thing[s] I learned is that, everyone wants to help, most people just don't know how and don't know about what's going on. ... I barely knew anything about what's going on and how to help before I entered [this class], I still know less than most people, but still more than most adults. Most adults don't know anything about it, those business owners were flabbergasted when we told them about what's happening and how they can help. They didn't teach this in schools back then, but they do now and kids are the ones who are getting the education that will help change the world.

Pursuing the Critical Edge

Integrative curriculum defined in this way is the most generative of the approaches and may pose the most challenge to teachers. This approach represents the "critical edge" of local learning that is currently causing so much excitement in some communities. When students, teachers, and members of the community work on this "edge," the purpose of a study grows from content acquisition to framing the democratic engagement for the student and provides the opportunity to enact social change.

An openness to structure schooling around the lives of students represents a critical view toward what should be taught in schools. In an effort to make sense of a series of shooting deaths in their neighborhood, students in Chicago (Stovall, Calderon, Carrera, & King, 2009) undertook an oral history project to find some answers. They interviewed residents and examined the media that had covered the shootings. One student reflected: "*I think we live in an ok community ... no neighborhood is perfect. I understand we have violence in our community but rich White communities have problems too. [The media] makes the rest of the world look at us like we're bad people*" (Stovall, 2009, p. 55). Another student writes: "*Too many influences have changed our community like gang violence, drugs, and homicides. All these influences affect the younger generation from what they see as right and wrong*" (Stovall, 2009, p. 55). This level of

Tom Moore, City High School. Used with permission.

attention to how students learn and what they really experience reflects what can be termed the "critical edge" of local learning.

Detroit, ravaged by the demise of the auto industry that left conditions exacerbated by racism and governmental neglect, is unarguably one of the most devastated landscapes in America. Many in Detroit, rather than being pulled down by this despair, are seeing this time as an opportunity to rebuild the city and the educational system around the needs of people. Julia Putnam (2011) is one of the many community activists who fosters this more vibrant view of the future: "Families in cities across the country are hungry for the type of school where kids are useful, where hope goes up and crime goes down, and where kids are surrounded by people who will love them up" (p. 62).

The mission of Grace Lee Boggs School (http://boggsschool.org) that Putnam and colleagues founded in 2013, captures this forward energy. On the website, it says: "*Students deserve an education that respects their unique contribution to building our society. They are not seeking an education to get out of Detroit; they see their education as a means to make Detroit a wonderful place to live.*" Teachers at the school believe in the power of local investigations to get students out of the school and provide an opportunity to re-imagine a new way of learning and being in community.

In New Mexico, students play a significant role in revitalizing rural communities while exploring career possibilities (Pitzl, 2011). Through the New Mexico Revitalization Initiative (NMRI), strong community-school partnerships students gain the opportunity to work in and in some cases start their own businesses and build new skills of handcrafts, agronomy, carpentry, finance, and more. Five high school students in Roy experimented with transferring graphic images from computers to an electronic embroidery machine. The girls applied images to jeans, baseball caps, pillows, and other cloth items and with the support of NMRI grew into a permanent business in their town: the Rough and Tough Embroidery Company. Another group of students in the town of Loving worked with experienced trade workers (electricians, plumbers, etc.) to build low-cost, energy-efficient homes in the community. They received college support and entry to the construction industry with a waiver for the traditional five-year journeyman requirement. In this example, this work not only opened up career possibilities for students, but also directly impacted the economic vitality of the community.

> "This generation will require leaders and citizens who can think ecologically, understand the interconnectedness of human and natural systems and have the will, ability and courage to act."
>
> Michael Stone (2009, p. 4)

Integrative curriculum design is built around the question generated by the student, not the subject. The outcome in this approach is more related to a student's personal understanding of issues and larger questions of community renewal, although content acquisition is still part of this process. In the New Mexico project, the whole system opened up ways for students to be actively engaged in the community while exploring possible pathways to their futures. The questions can emerge from the students' authentic partnerships or their exploration of the place, or they may be initially articulated by the teacher. The focus is on what students need to do in order to address a particular issue. A teacher may have to track the learning as it happens rather than being able to map it out ahead of time.

Rob Riordan (2013) shares a rationale for putting subjects to better use:

> Why not study anthropology, zoology, or environmental science? Why not integrate art with calculus or chemistry with history? Why not pick up skills and understandings in all of these areas by uncovering and addressing real problems and sharing findings with authentic audiences? Why not invent a useful product that uses electricity or devise solutions to community problems, all the while engaging in systematic observation, collaborative design and public exhibitions of learning?

When students experience learning in the ways Riordan describes, they come to see the reasons for learning history, writing clearly, and interpreting scientific phenomenon. Integrative studies give subjects a clear purpose. These purposes emerge for the student and don't always need to be articulated by the teacher. While students can approach questions of great importance in discipline-specific studies, these larger purposes function more easily in an integrated approach.

> **"The essence of integration lies in the use of subject matter by the learner rather than by teachers."**
> William Smith (cited in Beane, 1997, p. 15)

People are mistaken when they think that incorporating a larger purpose into school studies weakens the knowledge mastered. To the contrary, when answers are pursued for a worthwhile purpose, students are motivated by the real reasons for being a historian, a writer, a mathematician, or an artist. They might be preserving the town's history, providing their community with a newspaper, calculating income that might be lost to outside companies, or revitalizing a neglected lot. They are doing the discipline, not reading about what others have done, and this often provides a more academically rigorous environment for learning.

Real Problems Emerge in Local Places

All kinds of "problems" emerge from places. The knowledge and experiences necessary to solve these problems may exceed both the discipline boundaries and the parameters of what is traditionally thought of as "schoolwork." When students become engaged in authentic problems, the solutions they pursue may not resemble traditional outcomes. The problem itself may require new information or dictate a different approach or level of analysis. New information is needed to solve the problem. A teacher says: "*We didn't start out to get involved with the Conservation Board of our town but that is what we needed to solve the problem.*"

When a teacher sets out to explore her town with her students, questions may emerge that go beyond what she anticipated. Students may ask about the history of the town and when the buildings were built and also unexpected questions, such as "*Why is my town poor? Why do so many young people leave when they are teenagers?*" If they are exploring stream bank erosion, they might ask: "*How come the houses down by the river are always the ones that are threatened in a flood?*" Questions emerge that challenge and inspire teachers to turn to the study of things that were not originally intended.

Jean reflects: "Why are we 'solving problems' in isolation from community? We close the door of a classroom [and work] within the confines of four walls. We create hypothetical problems ... when the world has no shortage of them." Many students experience homelessness, evictions, and displacement or live with the legacy of these events. Linda Christensen, an advocate for bringing student voice and experience to the center of education, writes of a project she co-taught with Dianne Leahy. They wanted students to learn about the many ways people of color have had their homes "stolen." Christensen (2012) writes:

> I can wax poetic about the importance of story in students' lives, but reading literature of poverty and despair without offering a historical explanation leaves students with little understanding about how things came to be the way they are. And that's worth writing and reading about.
>
> *(p. 13)*

During the yearlong unit titled "Stealing Home," they examined historical photographs, primary documents, and narratives and used writing to express their understanding of national events. At the end of the year, the teachers wanted to bring it back to the students' "parallel" histories and their own experiences of displacement. In Portland, Oregon, students explored the history of a vital black neighborhood that had been "cleared" to make way for a highway and other urban "improvements." When her students went to investigate Christensen (2013) advised: "Name the places. Name the buildings. Name the freeways. Name the stores. Get specific about the place and then use your feelings about loss to move your poem" (p. 39). A student named Uriah Boyd (2013, quoted in Christensen) wrote this poem:

The place that I call home is humble
And its creaky floorboards have seen us all
in our most vulnerable state.
Gramma and Grampa dancing
Barefoot in the living room,
the "shuffle shuffle" of their feet
becoming the musical selection of the evening.
These doorframes have held up dreams
Hoisted them upon their broad shoulders
and offered them up to the skies.
That front door has warmly greeted kind souls,
and the back has banished offenders.
I once mopped the floor with Mama's tears.
And the scent of Gramma's sweet
potato pie will forever haunt this kitchen ...
In the confines of these walls,
Three of my cousins were born.
And now you tell me that you want to take this place away
For the "greater good."
Whose good?

The June Jordan School for Social Equity in San Francisco (www.jjse.org) has a mission to include issues of social justice as part of their curriculum. The high school has a comprehensive structure in place to support the students' capacity for community engagement and ability to understand the many issues that challenge communities. One part of this structure was a class that met regularly to support the service work students were doing.

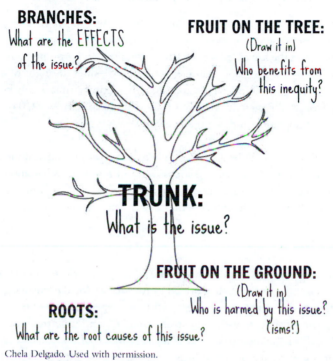

Chela Delgado. Used with permission.

Chela Delgado, who ran the seminar, used a tool called "Frierian trees." She said that "the branches were the outcomes of the problem but students had to dig down in their research to find its roots." The "trees of analysis" helped students clarify what part of the issue they wanted to address in their service projects. Students explored problems such as gang violence, dropouts, homelessness, and explored historical conflicts such as tourism versus homelessness and downtown development versus dockworkers that were explored in a book called *Towards Land, Work & Power* (Browne, Franco, & Williams, 2006), a political history of San Francisco. Chela remembers learning about the trees in a workshop:

> I thought the trees would be a good tool for determining community action projects because a student might start out thinking that she wanted to work on an issue like teenage pregnancy, and through the root cause analysis realize that she actually wanted to do a project around holistic sex education. Or students who wanted to work on gang violence eventually came to

realize that they really wanted to advocate for stronger sports programs in schools when they found the root problem might actually be lack of after-school activities for youth.

(personal communication, December 2, 2013)

"Kids will bring up the issues that need to be brought up."

Because authentic problems are solved in real places, teachers may find themselves paying attention to neighborhoods and issues that have traditionally been ignored. This often carries the learning into uncharted territory and prompts some rethinking of a subject's purpose. For example, oral history—often thought of as a technique to record the wisdom and experience of another time—can be used to better interrogate the present. Vermont folklorist Greg Sharrow (2004) invites us to think of ethnography in this more generative way:

> Oral history needn't be restricted only to older people and oral history projects don't necessarily have to focus only on the past. What about sending kids out into the community to explore "difference"—cultural, racial, religious, ethnic, class difference—the very difference that is so evidently present in most public schools.
>
> *(p. 5)*

The view toward the work students do in this way is Frierian in the sense that they are learning to "read their world" in order to act for the greater good. Just as Friere taught the basic skills of literacy within a larger purpose of understanding how the power structures were organized, teachers can frame traditional knowledge and skills of "schoolwork" within a larger frame of understanding how the world works and what role individuals can play. This sets the work of education in a larger context and puts students in situations where they can grapple with real problems. Students learn from and bring benefits to the community in which they live. Democracy is the purpose.

Students get a particular thrill from uncovering new answers to new questions. Who wouldn't? They like the challenge, the newness of the work, and the feeling that they are doing something worthwhile. A high school student working on a documentary about his town exclaimed, "We are uncovering the hidden story of our city!" Young learners have always suspected that there were better answers than the ones handed to them in school. What a surprise it is to them—and to their teachers!—when they finally get to dig for these real answers. Friere (1970) describes this energy:

> Students, as they are increasingly posed with problems relating themselves in the world and with the world, will feel increasingly challenged and obliged

to respond to that challenge. Because they apprehend the challenges as inter-related to other problems within a total context, not as a theoretical question, the resulting comprehension tends to be increasingly critical and less alienating. Their response to the challenge invokes new challenges, followed by new understandings; and gradually the students come to see themselves as committed.

(p. 81)

This commitment can be seen in large and small things; it depends on how real the work is. It comes when students address real issues like social justice and the more mundane aspects of life on earth. Kids can get excited when they discover a whole new way to think about what is literally under their feet. A student writes enthusiastically about soil bacteria: "Life or death dramas are unfolding beneath our feet every day. Countless super heroes—bacteria performing roles that make life itself possible—are ready to bring their untold tales to the public" (King Middle School, 2009).

Education for the Future

How to best "educate for the future" has had a muddled history in education. These days, it is most often used to suggest preparation for work or college readiness—all in the name of global prosperity. Designing integrated curriculum in which students set their own course portrays a young person's preparation for the future differently. Looking forward to the future means paying better attention to the present. Students should be doing worthwhile work now, learning whatever attributes are important to being able to work peacefully and productively with others and discovering their own strengths. As a colleague said, "We are helping them shape this very moment, right now."

Learning to grapple with complex issues is a lifelong undertaking. Global warming, food security, clean water, economic equity—these huge problems need to be addressed by people who can analyze complex problems, understand interrelationships, and speak articulately. Our problems are huge webs of inter-actions. Think of what residents of the Gulf learned about corporate values in the aftermath of the oil spill in 2010. Consider what victims of flooding learn about the role of government. We need to understand environmental degradation not as single instances of pollution and redeemable "mistakes" but as they relate to the underlying assumptions about how we live on earth. Do people go hungry because there isn't enough food or is the distribution system unfair? Are these understandings important to learn in school? Might school be more about life?

Curricular undertakings can better align with real issues in many concrete ways. Consider the influence physical space can have on young people. While the

Sharon Danks. Used with permission.

society struggles with questions about energy, infrastructure, and renewable build-ing supplies, many go to school each day in buildings from a previous century that belie any commitment to green, energy-efficient, aesthetically pleasing design. "The campus can communicate that the school is a fortress designed to keep kids and the rest of the world out—or it can reveal itself as a place of wonder that draws children to appreciate their relatedness to the world," according to Stone (2009, p. 89). Students can be more directly involved in issues that directly relate to the physical environment in which they are learning.

When the work is truly embedded in the community, and reflect the issues that face society, the answers will not be confined to the classroom. Big issues are dealt with, real problems solved, and authentic partnerships forged. Students become problem solvers, civic agents, community leaders, and team members. They learn to see the whole of problems, not just the subject-isolated aspect of a problem.

A powerful template for exploring, understanding, and improving communities is presented by the *Healthy Neighborhoods, Healthy Kids Guide* (Tillman, 2007, p. 11) from Shelburne Farms, Shelburne, Vermont. All of this booklet and other curricu-lum resources created by the Sustainable Schools Project are available online (www. sustainableschoolsproject.org).

Healthy Neighborhoods/Healthy Kids Project Flow

1. STUDY NEIGHBORHOOD and PLACE
Students explore their relationship to, and the uniqueness of where they live. They reflect on what they know and how they feel about their neighborhood.

2. DEFINE QUALITY of LIFE
Students develop a list of quality of life features to define who and what contributes to a safe and healthy life for all. Students then decide which features they want to be the focus of their learning and community work and research topics related to those features.

3. CREATE NEIGHBORHOOD REPORT CARDS
Based on their quality of life research, students develop Report Cards that they will use to grade the current condition of specific neighborhood features.

4. CONDUCT A NEIGHBORHOOD WALK
Together with parents, volunteers, and community leaders, students explore their neighborhood to examine and document the condition of specific neighborhood features, using the report cards as a guide.

5. SHARE RESULTS
Students compile Neighborhood Walk findings and make recommendations for fixing or improving conditions they deem unsafe and unhealthful. They share these results with appropriate community members, officials, and organizations through presentations, letter writing, or report writing.

6. PLAN A PROJECT
Students choose and implement a neighborhood improvement project (or projects) that addresses report card findings and recommendations.

7. CELEBRATE and REFLECT
Students organize and hold a community celebration where they honor and acknowledge their participation in making a difference in their community.

Shelburne Farms. Used with permission.

Education for Sustainability

One of the ways that teachers take the larger questions of life and weave them into curricular purposes is called "education for sustainability." It is a compelling practice that instills the purpose of education within the large ideas of sustainability as a way to understand our world and how we live on this planet for the long term. The interconnecting issues of the environment, social justice, and the economy become a frame for curriculum design that help us understand the world's complexity such as systems, cycles, change over time, and community. Sustainability provides a lens that anchors curriculum in place and service and is grounded in the belief that young people can make a difference in their world.

Coming to understand and grapple with big problems in local places generates understandings that have an impact on the learner and the community. Interconnectedness, systems thinking, quality of life, and envisioning a desired future—students can observe, experience, and interact with these ideas. When understanding these larger phenomena is treated as an "enduring understanding," then the identified tasks and knowledge pose a more complex view of curriculum. Students experience the inner workings of systems in the places where they live, gain experience interpreting and applying knowledge in real settings, and find courage to explore ways to affect change. Such courage doesn't happen to grown-ups when it is time to be an adult. It develops in young people as they practice and have opportunities to act in bold and authentic ways with and for other community members. Students need, as one educator put it, a chance to strengthen their "civic muscles."

Issues that face us on a global scale emerge locally. In order for groups of people to effectively grapple with large issues, they cannot be tied to subject boundaries; large issues need to be confronted face-to-face, in their entirety.

> Through an integrated approach to curriculum that removes the artificial barriers between disciplines and content areas, EFS [Education for Sustainability] allows students ample opportunity to apply their understanding and knowledge to new situations through a problem- and project-based approach that is deeply rooted in place. Project-based, integrated curricula centered on real-world problems provide rigor and relevance and give students the opportunity to apply their prior learning from discrete content areas.
>
> *(Cirillo, Hoyler, & Kadden, 2013, p. 279)*

At the Sustainability Academy in Burlington, Vermont, all subject areas are steered toward the "big ideas" of sustainability that provide a frame for the K–5 curriculum. The following is an example of one year's plan for the essential questions addressed in each grade:

Kindergarten: What is community?
Grade 1: How are people and nature a community?
Grade 2: How does change happen in a system, and what strategies do people use to create change?
Grade 4/5: What makes a sustainable community? How do individuals' choices affect a sustainable community? (alternating years)

At the Al Kennedy School in Oregon (Smith, 2011), the curriculum addresses themes of architecture, energy, water, forests, and agriculture. Students learn about these human activities in the context of civic engagement and create energy-efficient, ecologically sound housing and take part in water restoration, forestry management, and food production. Exploring these big questions can trigger a new-found identity and sense of purpose. As one student said:

> If you come to this school, you'll not be a follower, you'll be a leader. That's pretty much prepping me for when I go out in the real world. I'll not be some person following around others; I'm going to be a leader out there saying, "hey, this is what's going on, this is what we need to do, let's get on it."
>
> *(quoted in Smith, 2011, p. 74)*

Looking backward and forward to come to understand the places we live requires a new level of participation. From a fifth-grader who speaks at a public forum outlining recommendations for more access to public play space or a middle-grade student mentoring a homeless younger child, to a high school student building a house for a homeless family, schools that immerse themselves in the issues of today are sparkling with youth that care, pay attention to their world, and are performing at high levels. The outcomes are significant.

★★★★★★★★★★

There is very often deep subject knowledge embedded in this work, but that is not the only outcome. For the student, it is not just knowing something but also doing something about it. The teacher is still able to offer useful feedback on all these dimensions of learning. She can give feedback on the student's writing or speaking skills. She can also offer feedback on ways that a student assumes responsibility, communicates effectively, and demonstrates what one teacher called "stick-to-it-ness." These are all traits that come to bear in a democratic life.

As mentioned in the beginning of Part II, the four approaches outlined in these chapters are seldom used in their pure form but rather serve as constructs and inspiration for the myriad of ways that teachers *engage the local*. There is a dance between experience, content, places, and personal agency that takes place when students learn deeply in the context of their communities. They learn science better, write better, learn history better, and develop reasons for using skills that they might have previously seen as drudgery. Alongside these tasks, they also learn how the world works and what their place in it might be.

★★★★★★★★★★

References

Beane, J. (1997). *Curriculum integration: Designing the core of democratic education.* New York, NY: Teachers College Press.

Birmingham Covington School. (2013). *Doing business in Birmingham.* Retrieved October 12, 2013, from the Doing Business in Birmingham Wiki: http://doingbusinessinbirmingham.wikis.birmingham.k12.mi.us/

Browne, J., Franco, M., & Williams, S. (2006). *Towards land, work & power: Charting a path of resistance to U.S.-led imperialism.* San Francisco, CA: Unite to Fight Press.

Christensen, L. (2012). Burned out of homes and history: Unearthing the silenced voices of the Tulsa race riot. *Rethinking Schools, 27*(1), 12–18.

Christensen, L. (2013). Stealing home: Eminent domain, urban renewal, and the loss of community. *Rethinking Schools, 27*(4), 34–41.

Cirillo, J., Hoyler, E., & Kadden, S. (2013). Educating for sustainability. In D. Rowe (Series Ed.), *Achieving sustainability: Visions, principles, and practices* (pp. 276–285). Detroit, MI: Macmillan Reference USA.

Freire, P. (1970). *Pedagogy of the oppressed.* New York, NY: Continuum.

King Middle School. (2009). *Windsor 7 gets their hands dirty in soil super heroes.* Retrieved August 30, 2010, from http://king.portlandschools.org/files/houses/w1/index.php

Pitzl, J. (2011). Revitalizing communities in New Mexico. *Phi Delta Kappan, 92*(6), 16–21.

Putnam, J. P. (2011). Another education is happening. *Monthly Review 63*(3), 56–63.

Riordan, R. (2013, January 17). Change the subject: Making the case for project-based learning [Web log message]. Retrieved February 22, 2014, from www.edutopia.org/blog/21st-century-skills-changing-subjects-larry-rosenstock-rob-riordan

Roberts, P. (2013). Doing business in Birmingham. *Green Teacher 99,* 9–11.

Sharrow, G. (2004). Discovering community: Ethnographic inquiry as a tool for community discovery. *Community Works Journal, 6*(2), 5, 29.

Smith, G. (2011). Linking place-based and sustainability education at Al Kennedy High School. *Children, Youth and Environments, 21*(1), 59–78.

Stone, M. K. (2009). *Smart by nature: Schooling for sustainability.* Healdsburg, CA: Watershed Media.

Stovall, D., Calderon, A., Carrera, L., and King, S. (2009). Youth, media, and justice: Lessons from the Chicago Doc Your Bloc Project. *The Radical Teacher, 86,* 50–58.

Tillman, T. (Ed.). (2007). Healthy neighborhoods, healthy kids guide [PDF publication]. Shelburne, VT: Shelburne Farms Sustainable Schools.

PART III

Planning for Local Learning

Logistics and Challenges

Rethinking where we learn is one of the most fundamental changes in thinking that teachers experience when *engaging the local*. As students search for answers to their questions in new and different places, teachers learn new ways to teach. These new sources of information are no longer always text-based but rather three-dimensional, breathing people, places, and local happenings. The view shifts from inside work that relies on printed text to outside work with live happenings. A new view emerges of where learning might and can happen and what is important to learn. The break away from traditional text unhinges the work from the confines of the pages—and onto the streets! In order to reorient learning toward these more vibrant "texts," teachers must let go of many ingrained patterns of schooling and come to see the new possibilities all around.

In a somewhat overstated but enduring view of traditional education, the teacher is seen at the front of the room, guiding students through information and tasks. After the student learns to read, the teacher's job is to help students navigate through many written sources such as textbooks, historical documents, encyclopedic/web information, and works of fiction. The teacher poses well-worn questions that prompt a student response in the form of essays, research papers, personal responses, and short answers. The students' role is to extract from the text what the teacher—and others before her—have determined to be meaningful "answers." Classroom dialogue echoes a familiar refrain of: *"Where is the answer? Here on this page!"* In contrast, when students pursue authentic questions, the teacher is alongside the students, headed out the door, saying, *"Where will we find the answer to this question?"*

While the contrast may seem overstated to some, it sadly is not. Not only are many schools and classrooms entrenched in well-worn patterns—the contrast is accentuated in some poorer schools where teachers experience less options. The weight of high-stakes testing creates pressure that thwarts a teacher's capacity to deliver rich, authentic curriculum, hinders the joy and breadth of learning for the student (Meier, 2003), and keeps teachers and students locked in to a predominantly text-based experience.

This contrast is not to say that traditional texts do not have an important role in authentic investigations. Even when teachers become fully immersed in the learning opportunities outside of school, traditional texts can—and should—remain an integral part of the work that students do. Friere writes of this as a fluid partnership:

> Reading the world always precedes reading the word and reading the word implies continually reading the world. [. . .]This movement from the word to the world is always present, even the spoken word flows from our reading of the world. In a way . . . we can go further and say that reading the word is not preceded merely by reading the world, but by a certain form of writing it, or rewriting it . . . of transforming it by means of conscious, practiced work. For me, this dynamic movement is central to the literacy process.
>
> *(Friere & Macedo, 1987, p. 35)*

Friere's union of the written word and the three-dimensional world compels us to view where we live as places that can be read, interpreted, interrogated, and deciphered. This view invites us to think of "place of text" and deepens our view of the ways that we can *read* our world. When teachers consider ways to engage students, they talk about getting them out of their chairs, out of the classroom, out of the school building, and away from the traditional patterns of schooling. This continual search for a more active, engaged way to teach is an enduring aquifer that brings refreshment and renewal to stagnant practices.

Ideally, we can find ways to use authentic printed texts in more meaningful ways alongside the layered texts of places nearby. Indeed, as Friere instructs, *the reading of the word* goes hand in hand with the reading of the world.

Currently, the Common Core has offered teachers an opportunity to consider "complex text." This can be an opportunity to enrich the content and types of printed text we share with our students as well as an opening to more broadly define the texts that will help us understand our complex world. Places, people, and things can perplex, instruct, and add new dimensions to the ways that students experience printed text. We need a balance where the purpose of an authentic, meaningful, and democratic education drives the choosing of experiences—both inside and outside of the classroom.

Part III examines the logistics and challenges of how teachers use real, vibrant texts—the people, places, and events that surround our classrooms to design rich learning opportunities. Chapter 7 presents ways that teachers can plan for and better use the environment outside of school as sites for learning. Chapter 8 shares the ways teachers can use the design tools of *Understanding by Design* (Wiggins & McTighe, 1998, 2005) to incorporate the more fluid interactions between the learner and the community as planned learning activities.

TEACHER PORTRAIT #6
JUDY ELSON
MIDDLE

"Not Just a Walk in the Woods"

Judy Elson teaches in a beautiful classroom—not because of state of the art resources but because her whole western wall of windows faces a wide span of woods and fields, with a peek of Lake Champlain and a view toward New York's Adirondacks in the distance. "I can point right there . . . when talking about plate tectonics, weather systems, natural beauty—it's all right there."

An experienced environmental educator who worked for many years at Shelburne Farms (Shelburnefarms.org), it is fitting that Judy have all these riches at her door. She teaches in the small town near where she lives and spends a lot of time with her family enjoying the lake and woods. She voices concern at how little her students know about the natural world and seeks out ways to use the curriculum to bring them closer to nature in what she calls her "natural classroom."

She puts a lot of thought into learning outside the classroom and asks, "What will be the best use of our time?" Although she is well trained at this and likes doing it, she comments that it takes a long time to design learning experiences outside. "You need to be able to show what you get done because it's a lot of bus time and that's expensive, so we need to make it worthwhile. I like trying to make those connections for kids . . . not just go for a walk in the woods. It's not a walk in the woods." "We work when we are outdoors, we have field journals. There's information they're looking for. There is some exploring but it's exploring with a purpose. She finds ways to search out how ideas in the science book play out in the natural world on a regular basis. [We might] dig in the soil pit, observe fungi, search for animal tracks and key leaf patterns."

As practiced as she is in learning outdoors, Judy acknowledges the challenges: "It's harder to have control of student work . . . in the field. Kids are spread out [. . .] doing different things at one time. That challenges some teachers more than others—it's beyond their comfort zone." Also some students are challenged being outdoors. "They may come from a class that never went outdoors. I set guidelines the first day we go out [and make clear] that the habitat is the classroom just as much as in here and if you have problems outside, I can still send you to the principal. Or they realize that if they misbehave they will miss out. "And no one ever doesn't want to go [. . .]. I've never had a kid not want to go."

"They know it's going be a good time [and that] it's something different than sitting in this classroom at these tables and these four walls." The large windows in Judy's room beckon constantly, and she often heeds the call, taking her students to learn the things that she feels she cannot teach them inside.

7

PLACE AS TEXT

Teachers view the textbook as an archetypal symbol of traditional education and often pose the new work they are doing in contrast to using printed text. "It's less predictable," one says, "not like a textbook." While textbooks play a useful role in many ways, and rich (printed) texts can serve a prominent role in inquiry, the over-reliance on printed sources, and textbooks in particular, stands in contrast to ways teachers come to see "place as text." This illustrates a profound shift as teachers change their view of what sources are worthy and invite a wide array of "texts" for students to engage with. This chapter examines some of the fundamentals of how teachers use these new texts as students conduct investigations outside of the classroom.

The call to make education more "authentic" and "real-world" is not a new refrain in the history of American education. The swing to and fro from progres-sive to traditional has characterized the debate for more than 100 years (Cuban, 2000). Thinking of "place as text" is a reissue of Dewey's (1938) invitation from many years ago:

> [In traditional education] . . . the school environment of desks, blackboards, a small school yard was supposed to suffice. . . . There was no demand that the teacher should become intimately acquainted with the conditions of the local community, physical, historical, economic, occupational etc. *in order to utilize them as educational resources.*
>
> *(p. 40, emphasis added)*

> *"I want it to be part of them forever. When we just do the books?*
> *They forget it in a month."*

Learning means more when students go directly to the source. During an interview, Jean commented that when his students gather the stories from the people who lived through them, it "teaches students where history comes from. It doesn't just appear in a textbook." His comment prompted us to think about how it was like wanting students to know where their food comes from: *Farms! Dirt! Fields! Not the grocery store!* Knowledge comes "straight from the land where it is grown." Students seek knowledge in the places where subjects begin. They can experience an original event through scientific inquiry, interviews, data analysis, observation, and dialogue. Subjects become useful tools—in the eyes of the students—to comprehend complex issues of the day. "I never understood globalization before," says one student who studied its local implications. "But when I interviewed the local merchant and heard what he had to say about the things he ordered from all over the world, it started to make sense to me." In getting close to the original sources, students are able to see that it is their history that is important and their environmental problems that might be solved. As their studies take on more meaning, they become more active observers and participants in the world around them.

Place as Text

In much of education, one of the first decisions teachers make is in regard to what texts she will use. She thinks about what she wants her students to learn and what readings will help them learn it. It is a fundamental question when planning a learning experience.

It is still about choosing texts. However, as teachers experience ways students learn from different sources, they get a wider view of what might be useful information and where sites of learning might be. The "texts" that teachers choose include what is happening in communities.

> *"Talking to people, interviewing, listening . . . [it is] knowledge from*
> *all different sources . . . it works."*

When teachers take a critical stance toward learning in the community, there are no limits to what can serve as sources of knowledge. The teacher arranges—and makes space for the student to arrange—connections with other people, places, and forms of knowledge. As a designer of professional learning opportunities, I marvel at how we keep pushing our view of what counts as a learning site. I might find myself standing around a storm drain, talking about where the water goes with a city planner, examining an old railroad bed and considering what was transported 100 years ago, piecing together commercial patterns from clues on historic buildings. It is a new kind of learning and because it is often a puzzle, it can engage the learner in ways that the printed page cannot.

As students follow their questions, previously unconsidered sources of knowledge provide new understandings. A light bulb might be a source of inquiry as the student traces local evidence of the path from incandescent bulbs to the time when gaslights lit neighborhoods. Things that may not have been thought of as "academic" become a valued pathway to learning. Things such as city pipes, the slope of a roof, or an old bridge might become the focus of a student's investigation. Experiences such as city council meetings, public forums, and debates over land use become part of the educational agenda. Different people come to be viewed as experts. The problem itself may steer the learner to a new "text."

A teacher will not always know what her students will find or what action it might inspire them to take. A teacher asks, "How can you know what questions emerge when you put a group of fifth-graders in charge of earthworms?" Another teacher takes her students outside to dig a soil pit: "I have some idea that I will find a lot of clay and that it might be wet this time of year, but I never really know what is going to be down there." Exploring a city street a teacher says: "We don't know who will be out on the sidewalks that day. It is sometimes a surprise to all of us! We need to learn to bring the 'out' in!"

It is a challenge for teachers that the "texts" are not always chosen ahead of time. It is possible for a teacher to use a primary document or bridge site or involve an elder to structure a known outcome. Yet, often, *turning outward* involves this element of uncertainty. When students do authentic research in their communities, they come to spend more time "looking out" rather than "looking up" information because the answers are out in the community. The original discovery ignites different responses and more questions. It opens up the classroom to the possibility that learning can become more of a shared enterprise with others.

This same well-worn pathway is played out in web-based research. Asking students to research online is not more real than papered text, but it can be. Its authenticity depends on the extent to which the reader can become a critical consumer of the information. Although much of the information on the Internet can be fresher, most of it is still text. The quantity of it means that the student needs to be alert to its quality. Critical consumption of online information can lead to many authentic connections—such as finding local peacekeepers or keepers of bees or the location of historical documents.

People as Sources of Knowledge

> *"We invite the community to come in and each person brings their own richness . . . and then we learn things from them."*

When Elliot Wigginton, founder of Foxfire, an inspirational educational project in Rabun Gap, Georgia, sent kids out to explore the hidden and underappreciated treasures of that Appalachian region, it was not clear what they were going to find. However, he had an openness to his surroundings and, as Foxfire grew, an abiding faith in what might be around the next turn. In *Sometimes a Shining Moment*

(1985), he describes the day a student named Patsy came up to him after class and said, "I've got a relative you might want to interview. She still lives in the old way and knows how to do all the stuff you all are talking about. I'll introduce you to her if you want." Wigginton writes: "One thing you learn in this business is never to pass up an introduction," so he asked three students to go with Patsy and check it out. A few days later, one of the students reported: "You'll never believe this one. . . ." Wigginton (1985) continues:

> That weekend at the students' insistence I got the tape recorder [and we] drove into Macon County, over several miles of gravel roads and finally ended up on a deeply rutted dirt and mud driveway that ended on the side of a mountain in the yard of an unchinked log house with stone chimneys and a tin roof. Getting no answer at the front door, we walked around to the kitchen and found Aunt Arie, in her eighties, all alone, working with a paring knife, to scrape the hair and bristles from a severed head of a huge hog.
>
> *(pp. 127–128)*

Aunt Arie was to become a very important friend to Foxfire and the story of "finding her" illustrates Wigginton's view to the unknown treasures waiting to be discovered in the mountains surrounding his school. This meeting did not happen because of a preconceived or elaborate plan on his part; he did not know what he was going to find when he and his students went looking. Yet his willingness to explore what was outside the classroom dovetailed with how he saw his "job" as a language arts teacher and his ability to "follow the honey" when an opportunity for further learning presented itself.

If the hills of Appalachia give us an archetypal tale of community inquiry, the Llano Grande Center (www.llanogrande.org) is a modern-day parable. Francisco Guajardo (2007), a local educator who recognized the disconnection many Latinos felt toward their home and their own futures, sought ways to explore the assets of his South Texas community. He asked his students to conduct oral interviews. These efforts grew into a thriving enterprise with results not only in higher college attendance and academic success but powerful personal testimonies of their experiences. Guajardo's vision was to help students discover the hidden stories that revealed their true history: "People's stories, I have learned, are the richest material any teacher can use for instruction, for personal development, and even for transforming a community. Knowledge, spirit, and inspiration come from people, not from books" (p. 30).

One of the residents the students interviewed was 97-year-old Don Isabel Gutiérrez. Returning for their third visit, Guajardo tells of when they asked Don Isabel to talk about the town founders. Don Isabel states that he is a founder. A student politely asked: "What do you mean by that, Don Isabel? Wasn't the founder Edward C. Couch?" Don Isabel replied: "*No, no, no, joven . . . mira, tú has tomado agua en esta pueblo?*" ("No, no, no young man . . . listen, have you ever drunk water in this town?") When the student replied that he had, Don Isabel said that in 1926 he dug the ditches to lay the water pipes to bring water to Edcouch. "*Yo soy fundador de Edcouch*" ("I am the founder of Edcouch"), he proudly proclaimed (p. 27).

These live sources have lessons to teach that the printed page cannot, such as those gained by middle-level students with the Montana Heritage Project (www.montanaheritageproject.org). Umphrey (2007) reflects on the findings of students who had interviewed elders about their local history in a report to the local lumber company:

> The students said they had begun their study because they were depressed about the future and thought that they might find some answers by examining the past. But after researching decades of what seemed to be nonstop economic troubles, the kids concluded their presentation with this insight: "We looked to Libby's past for answers to our current troubles. But we didn't find answers. What we found was that life had always been difficult, but that our grandparents and great-grandparents had always found a way to help each other and to get through hard times. And so will we."
>
> *(p. 8)*

Steve Glazer (2004) believes students are "nestled in a living web of . . . primary and secondary sources, community elders, places, wisdom holders" and sees community explorations as the way to let students in on what he calls "the big secret . . . that the world itself is alive, infinitely rich and a teacher without peer" (p. 8). Anne comments: "I think it helps kids to not only know the geography and the river and what is unique about the place physically . . . but what is unique about the place through the human beings who live there. What kind of contributions do they make?" Students meet, talk, and share ideas with people who have different areas of expertise. A relationship develops with the people in the community. Sharyl notes:

> I think of it as a partnership. [And] it isn't just a partnership between me and my students. It's . . . between me and my students and people in the community. I'm bringing other adults into the classroom or . . . in the field with us, wherever they happen to be. Kids are working with people who are not the teacher and they value their expertise because they need to know what those people know to get the job done.

When the students in Kate's class watched and discussed the movie they had made about diversity in their community, they spoke about how making the film had changed how they felt about the residents of their community. One student reflected: "You can't just go by what you see; you have to learn what other people experience. You have to know what they have been through." When students have real problems to solve—*problems that other people have lived through*—the learning is propelled toward people with different life experiences. A student in Brownington, Vermont, comments on the significance of her research:

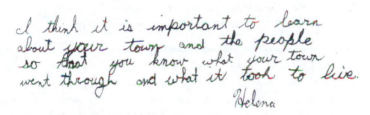

I think it is important to learn about your town and the people so that you know what your town went through and what it took to live.
Helena

Old Stone House Museum, Orleans County Historical Society. Used with permission.

Bringing in a guest speaker becomes a "lesson." A teacher prepares her students (and the guest) for the visit, facilitates the dialogue, and assesses what her students learned. I used to take time for the students to write thank-you notes to the people who visited our class. These were the "outcomes" of the lesson that I read and learned from. Often students identified specific knowledge and new understandings—as well as new questions and ideas about subsequent activities.

Places as Sources of Knowledge

All places have stories to tell. A teacher might organize a foray into the local woods and ask students to find examples of interdependence and interrelationship. An art teacher might take her students to a new place outside of school to create a mural. Holding a discussion or activity that helps students interpret the possibilities of the place is the first part of her plan. When exploring change in another neighborhood, a teacher might assign an open question such as: "Interview someone who remembers this block 20 or more years ago." Responses might include opinions about housing, jobs, social gatherings, and forgotten traditions. To find the stories, students need to pay close attention to the details of a place. Liberty Hyde Bailey's (1909) advice from 100 years ago for observing nature pertains to all places:

> Nature-study begins with the concrete, as the child does if left to itself. The child should first see the thing. It should then reason about it. Having a concrete impression, it may then go to the book to widen its knowledge and sympathies. Having seen mimicry in the eggs of the aphis on the willow or apple twig, or in the walking-stick, the pupil may then take an excursion with Wallace or Bates to the tropics and they see the striking mimicries of the leaf-like insects. Having seen the wearing away of the boulder or the ledge, he may go to Switzerland with Lubbock and see the mighty erosion of the Alps. Now and then the order may be reversed with profit, but this should be the exception, not the rule. From the wagon to the star should be the rule.
>
> *(p. 32)*

"Place-based learning brings students out of black and white books into a full-spectrum world of color."

Teachers who get kids out of the school building believe in the power of places to tell stories. The lessons of "nature-study" can be applied to all places. A history teacher speaks of the power of exploring the remains of a historic site with his students "to walk where they walked." Rob Hanson (2004) uses "power spots," a term he credits to Joseph Cornell, as opportunities for powerful lessons and a framework for personal interpretation. He contemplates the lessons that they might learn: "A rock might teach you about patience or firmness. Ants might demonstrate cooperation or determination" (p. 14). In the same focused way, a student might ponder a city street and ask: *"Why does everyone live so close together? I wonder how they get along?"*

Teachers who seek authentic learning experiences find ways for students to meet directly with other people and places. The teacher is no longer the only one who holds the knowledge to impart to the student. She becomes an intermediary between her students and a wide world with real problems and dilemmas.

> Place-based approaches recognize that learning is way more than words on a page. It is water moving around our boots, it's mud and cold. It's all those sensory dimensions in the real world we're part of. If its rivers kids

are learning about, then standing in one and turning over stones to find stoneflies, for instance, teaches in new ways . . . They gain new respect for the river and [come] to see themselves as part of something with a long history and a long future. They become more hopeful.

(Quinn as quoted in Clark, 2008, p. 43)

Steven Levy (1996) describes the many hidden topics that emerge when teachers turn to the places outside their schools in *Starting from Scratch: One Classroom Builds Its Own Curriculum:*

. . . A grain of wheat, a strand of wool, the shoes we wear and the name of our town have all led to exciting learning projects. I feel a special call to *mine the extraordinary out of the everyday* [emphasis added]. Familiar objects that [we] take for granted are filled with intrigue and meaning when we explore their origins.

(p. xvi)

One of Levy's projects was a yearlong study of his town's bike path (Levy & MacGowan, 1996). Bowman Elementary School (1994) students studied all aspects of the bike path throughout the year and published a book that was sold locally, titled *On the Path*. The focus and organization of the book developed from what the students chose to learn about the bike path, not content related to subjects. Some excerpts provide a flavor of what these fourth-graders learned:

Chapter 2: **The Bike Itself** explores the history of bicycling worldwide. "The bicycle has improved over 200 years. People will think back to our day, just as we have laughed at the strange-looking bicycles of 200 years ago, they may laugh at the best racing bicycles of today."

(p. 17)

Chapter 3: **History: Before the Bikeway** explains how the path came to be. "In the 1960s, the people of Massachusetts wanted fewer cars to drive to the city to minimize air pollution. This gave people the idea of converting the railroad tracks to a commuter bikeway."

(p. 23)

Chapter 4: **Planning** explains the community's planning process. " . . . If you think back, the bikeway was not always there. And before they built the bikeway, they had to plan it. . . . It took 15 years to plan but only 2 years to build. The bike path took seven more times as long to plan as to build."

(p. 25)

Other chapters are titled "Construction," "Costs," "Users," "Environment," "Abutters to the Bikeway," "Business," and "Safety." The last chapter, titled "Heart of the Bike Path," reads:

> This chapter is all about the feeling of the bikepath. . . . Luckily there is a peaceful path. What could be better than a path of talking, laughing, joyous people? It is so peaceful there in the warm summer evenings, the sun setting as the birds twitter, it relieves you from the business of the day, and it is a great way to get exercise. . . . As you ride through beautiful scenery you will feel like a child again.
>
> *(pp. 71–72)*

How to Plan Meaningful Learning outside the Classroom

A pre-service teacher once asked me, "How can you go outside when you have to stay inside and do the curriculum?" His frustration reflects a commonly held view that learning outside the classroom is "extra" and an "add-on." Yet well-crafted field experiences can engage students directly with all the essential questions humans experience. They can explore properties of water, interdependence of living things, human justice, sources of poetry . . . the possibilities are endless. The field work becomes worthwhile when the experience is woven in to the intent of your study.

Questions frame a field experience and clarify the learning challenge for students. It takes time to develop a clear focus and prepare students to "read" a place: *"Is this true? Does this really happen? How many cars go by? Who uses public transportation? Where are the safe places near our school?"* What questions do they have in advance and what questions will emerge from the field experience?

"Being there is best."

Students find it challenging to learn in new settings. They are used to learning in one way and learning in the field requires them to learn differently. A teacher muses on the need to:

> . . . train students to stop, listen, feel, observe, slow down, and internalize what is right around them—they won't think of doing it. They're too planned and busy and stressed. Once they're in the habit . . . it will be like a peaceful friend they will always think of visiting . . . when their mind and body are in need.

A high school student preparing for a field trip said: "It's a lot easier to learn here where we're used to it," as she pointed to the traditional accoutrements of school. . . . "I have my desk, my notebook, my backpack. . . . It all just feels more normal here." Her teacher addressed these concerns by taking time to discuss what was going to be needed on-site and what distractions there might be (such as traffic noises or construction).

> *"The deeper you can go outside the school walls . . . the deeper learning happens."*

Steve Glazer (2004) notes [for younger learners]: "Kids are creatures of habit. Their expectation is that outdoors equals recess." He makes suggestions on how teachers can help them focus:

> Special spots get students apart and settle their energy . . . [Use] writing and drawing prompts . . . Don't let them free-range; draw buildings, GPS trails, track animals, collect data off of tombstones, ID and age trees . . . whatever you do, make it meaningful, focused work that allows students to slow down, look closely and move into the space where discovery learning and insight happen.
>
> *(p. 11).*

There are many challenges for teachers and students when considering ways to take students into the field. While at first glance—it is about the logistics (scheduling, time, and money) teachers have to negotiate many relationships to extract students from the regular schedule. Clarifying our purposes is essential to making these negotiations more successful. Presented here are some commonly heard concerns about field experiences:

LEARNING IN THE FIELD: QUESTIONS AND CHALLENGES

How can I plan a field trip and still remain open to the unexpected?
It is not possible to overprepare for a field trip. That doesn't mean that you can't make changes once you arrive but it is always good to have a detailed plan when traveling off-site with a number of young people. I found this helpful when an unexpected encounter set off the schedule; it was a lot easier to see how to quickly adjust times so we would make it back on the bus!

How can I get kids out when it disrupts the schedule—there is no time!
Some schools have more fluid schedules than others. Schools that are stretched thin and share staff among different buildings have a harder time adjusting the schedule. The earlier you can share your plans with school officials and colleagues, the better chance you have to work out the details and get the flexibility and participation you need.

Arrange for whatever additional support is needed for students with special needs regarding safety, movement, or discipline. (Although in regard to matters of discipline, it is a commonly held opinion of many place-based educators that many behavior problems lessen when students are actively engaged outside of school!)

Give families all necessary information early. This includes the dates, any information on early departures or late arrival, and a heads-up on packed lunches, any special gear needed, and any upcoming fundraising events.

Often times you don't need to take your whole class out at once. You might have a willing community member or parent that would donate one afternoon a week to taking small groups out to explore. Older students can conduct many kinds of field investigations in self-directed groups or during time in flexible scheduling.

What about the high cost of field trips?

There is no question that the costs of getting out of school are often prohibitive. While this is the first thing that teachers think about, and sometimes it is too overwhelming to move beyond, there are ways to address the question of cost. Consider the following: walking field trips, community partnerships that support or contribute the cost, incorporating field experiences into your annual budget, and fundraising.

When fundraising, be specific about your needs. People would rather donate for specific things such as garden or cooking tools, admission to a science museum or art supplies for a community mural than non-specific goals such as "field trips" or "enrichment."

If I can't get outside, do I have any other choices?

Lisa Lusero (2006) suggests that there are "gradations of real" and names four ways to make learning more authentic: "interacting with the real thing; interacting with evidence of the real thing, interacting with something comparable to the real thing and linking the real thing to something with which we interact" (p. 58). She believes this does not always mean learning outside of the classroom; it often can be about bringing the outside in, both in verbal or actual instances of community connections.

Use technology to get places you can't get to. I am not in favor of virtual learning in the place of getting out of the school building, but I strongly support it as a way to deepen the investigations underway. There are numerous ways for small groups of students to capture information and share digitally—cutting down on the challenges of getting all students out of school.

In a workshop, I listened to two teachers discuss the challenges of getting outdoors with students. One was a veteran teacher of 15 years who averaged 15–20 field trips a year, and the other was contemplating taking her students outdoors for the first time. The new teacher was awestruck at the logistics the more experienced teacher was sharing. Nothing had prepared her to consider the planning involved in taking the learning outdoors. All the information she was hearing about safety, group dynamics, scaffolding the lesson, and arranging for materials seemed new and overwhelming. "I thought that all I had to think about was getting money for the buses," she said.

Fundraising, without a change in outlook toward learning in the field, is not a good use of time and energy. While there is some value in students helping to earn money for their adventures and for others in need, it is not the responsibility of students nor their teachers to garner funding for their education. Learning to collect pennies, host a bake sale, and wash cars are all worthy activities. Although not the reality, education—which includes the investigation of places outside of school—should be fully funded.

"I need to get them out; that is where the learning happens."

The real challenge of fundraising is educating others to the worth of learning outside the classroom. Consider proposing the cost of busses in place of textbooks in your budget, a suggestion that may feel insulting to teachers who no longer have a budget for textbooks. When the energy builds around the work young people do outside of school, oftentimes solutions for funding come. Partnerships with local business and community organizations can often become a source of support.

Teachers are apprehensive about leaving the classroom to learn. I took kids out a lot, and I always had a moment (usually right before I got on the bus) when I longed for the quiet calm of our classroom. "Let's go back inside and draw some maps," I would whisper to my teammate. However, it feeds you. A veteran teacher recalls the moment that convinced him for good of the value of getting out with students:

> You get to see the kids out there doing things that are genuine . . . especially the kids that struggle. Once I went out in the woods for a night walk and [this one student] laid down in the snow at 10 PM in the middle of winter in the national forest and loved it. He said: "This is the best thing I have ever done in my life."

Planning Pre-, On-Site and Post Learning (POP!)

Learning outside of the classroom is much more than "just" a field trip. It is an intentional engagement with places that involves a high level of planning and structured learning. Engagements in the field can be thought of as meeting up with new text. Just as there are considerations for the printed text pre-, during, and after reading, so too do field experiences benefit from pre- (P), on-site (O), post- (P) planning (POP!) (Demarest, 1997). The chart (Figure 7.1) presents some different ways to structure field experiences.

Pre-visit Considerations

The teacher is responsible for what students need to know before leaving the classroom. Just as any well-crafted lesson has a clear focus known to the students ahead of time, successful field experiences include well-articulated and shared expectations. A good teacher won't begin a lesson on long division without

"POP" (Pre-visit, On-site, and Post-visit)
PRE-visit: What do you want your students to know before you go?

Suggestions:
- Create the agenda with your students
- Plan and discuss all possible logistics.
- Share maps of where you will be going/with different perspectives (i.e., Google Earth).
- Have students make maps/outlines that they can add to on-site/GPS.
- Discuss with students the challenge of learning in a different environment/be clear about what you are going to ask them to do (process and outcome).
- Discuss any social considerations in regard to the people they will meet.
- Do some of the research ahead of time to develop questions and know what they need to find out on-site.
- Research your site and have students verify findings on-site.
- Give students plenty of time to practice any new technical skills they will use on-site.
- Clarify what they will need to bring with them (and for younger students/how they will carry it).
- Prepare for any safety considerations: What is there (access, weather, etc.), and what are the needs of your students (allergy, snacks, mobility).
- *Give students responsibility for success of the field trip.*

ON-site: What do you want your students to learn while they are there?

Suggestions:
- Devise a plan to address and amend questions that students brought to the site.
- Consider the use of pre-determined templates or captions to guide data and image collection.
- Have students act out their understanding of site *in situ.*
- Conduct interviews, video, collect data.
- Use of digital tools to capture images and audio.
- Ethnographic interrogation of site.
- What service opportunities are there on-site?
- Structure the gathering of data.
- Verify or confirm pre-conceived expectations.
- Use drawing or photography as a way to closely observe your surroundings.
- Use social media to write "wish you were here" messages.
- Confirm as group that you have gathered necessary information from the field.
- Use of video camera/audio.
- Be aware of protocol for collecting images of other people without permission.
- *Make the learning experience worthwhile, not just a "tour."*

POST-visit: What do you want your students to consider/learn after the visit?

Suggestions:
- Have students draw, post, or record a single memory.
- Use site as "story starter"—what (historical or geographically) accurate details can you add to your story now?
- Write a news story for the school newspaper or blog about the trip.
- Bring one image from the trip and add it to an album.
- Create monologues that tell the story from a specific perspective (i.e., "talking" building, rollerblade, or boat).
- Add information to Google Maps or pre-planned templates.
- Write and illustrate a "postcard" about the trip.
- Share info with other students—at school, in other schools, online.
- Create meaningful threads into the curriculum.
- Explore ways that new learning will be used.
- *Make the learning last.*

FIGURE 7.1

Amy B. Demarest, Place-based Curriculum Design: Exceeding Standards through Local Investigations.
© Routledge, 2015.

reviewing some simple examples of dividing with whole numbers or start a lesson on chemical reactions without making sure her students are familiar with the properties of individual chemicals. Clarity of purpose is equally important when learning in the field. A new teacher reflects:

> You know what it is. It's the prep work. You set the expectations very clear[ly] and make the task valuable . . . and when you do, they believe it's valuable and important and so they follow through with it and stay engaged.

Like any skilled teacher introducing students to new text, there is often new "vocabulary" to learn before going into the field. We would not ask our students to start a new book or article without some context, nor would we send students out to interview elders about a certain time in history without background knowledge. An English teacher prepares students to explore social justice in the community by asking, "Who benefits? Who loses?" Before heading out, students might examine instances of injustice in history, literature, and their own lives to better understand what they are looking for. This preparation gets them ready to seek answers to complex questions.

In *Healthy Neighborhoods, Healthy Kids Guide* (Tillman, 2007), fourth- and fifth-graders learn four key terms: neighborhood, community, quality of life, and indicators. These terms bring focus to the curriculum and are integral to the learning that the students do in this program. Anne (See Teacher Portrait #7), who has taught this curriculum shares that "these words can be a tangle. If we spend time with them ahead of time then they can see them in context and be better users of the words when we go out." Classroom learning becomes a "pre-text" activity prior to meeting up with the real-world manifestation. In subsequent activities, students develop a deep understanding of these words through research, collaboration, and action. They conduct surveys of their neighborhoods and develop criteria they deem "indicators" of a healthy community. Knowing these words gives them tools to interpret the nearby "texts" that are under consideration.

Teachers prepare students for the newness of a field experience by sharing information with them ahead of time. The more students know about a site before they go, the better. They won't be wasting precious brain activity when they get off the bus trying to figure out where they are. Maps, schedules, and tasks are all more useful when communicated ahead of time. Sharyl develops the schedule with her students that they then prepare and explain to parent chaperones.

Michael Winerip (2012) reports on a strategy called "trips to the sidewalk" used by Dao Krings, a second-grade teacher in New York City. Krings relies on real-world experiences to provide important background knowledge for developing literacy skills. It is an approach endorsed by her district that takes "a different tack" than the traditional advice from some educational experts who advise more reading at earlier ages. Krings's students visited an auto repair shop where one of her students sat in a car for the first time. "I sat in the front seat and then I sat in the back seat," he exclaimed. Another day, they studied parking meters and calculated the costs and logistics of using them and learned new vocabulary such as parking and violation. They also learned that a sign that said "No Standing Any Time" did not apply to second-graders standing on the sidewalk.

The next trip was to a parking garage. Before leaving, Mrs. Krings led her students through the process of predicting what they might see before they went— a strategy she compared to pre-reading a text. Students discussed how the garage would work including when the drivers would pay, which they thought would happen as drivers entered the garage.

On-site Considerations

When Ms. Krings's students arrived at the parking garage, they watched the cars enter and the drivers press the button to obtain a ticket. They didn't see anyone pay money when they entered. When they were able to talk to the parking attendant, he told them that "they don't pay to get in; they pay to get out." "I knew it," chimed two students!

> "A pedagogy that uses the local place as a critical text and laboratory fundamentally changes the perceptions of what is valuable information and what is understood to be real work."
>
> (HGSE, 1999, p. 12).

I remember when a teammate opened my eyes to how much could happen on-site. We were learning about steam travel and planned to visit the 1906 ship *SS Ticonderoga* that sailed Lake Champlain and is on exhibit at the Shelburne Museum (www.shelburnemuseum.org). She suggested: "Let's have the students research the jobs on the Ti (purser, maid, cook, boiler room, etc.) and do skits while they are there—using the setting and related artifacts to research the work involved to run a 220-foot steamer." They did! Most of the morning students spent time conducting their on-site research into the artifacts "in-situ." We then toured the site and "met" the "workers" at different parts of the ship, who told us about their jobs. We learned how the artifacts were used and what the work entailed and heard exciting stories that had stood out for our students. While this obviously took some collaborating with museum staff, the results were outstanding. It was easy to see that the students probably learned much more about working on a 19th-century steamboat than they would have if we had simply walked through the ship. Drawing in museums, interviewing workers in their workplace, and gathering new data on-site is always more engaging than "just looking." When students continue their research and share their findings as part of the field visit, they become better able to interpret the site to others.

In general, teachers should seek ways to interrogate the site as rigorously as possible. Consider what can engage a student on-site. Ms. Krings's students had a problem they were working on. Students can draw, write, watch—whatever will help them more effectively become engaged. Consider ways to use social media to have students bring life to different places—such as imagining what people in a portrait gallery are thinking. Tweet the response alongside the image of the portraits!

Give your students time to explore, observe, think, and have fun! Sometimes enjoying the site like "real people" is important. Time to play in a park, eat a meal in a restaurant, hang out in a coffeehouse, and listen to music can all contribute to students getting a better understanding of a place. Think of ways that your students can work in small groups with a clear task rather than moving as a "listening glob" from one part of the site to the other. Have time to be quiet and observe what is going on. Your plan can differentiate; students can accomplish different things on-site—in similar ways to structuring a "jigsaw" reading of a text. Bring in experts and local residents. Rotate students through stations. Different areas of expertise can be built.

Consider what role technology will have on the field experience. For example, two or three students in each small group might carry ipads for recording and access to other texts. Not every student needs to be digitally connected . . . the point is to interrogate the place where you are. Make this aspect of field work clear with students and part of their planning process. Clarify what role each student will have and what tools they will need to perform the task.

Barry Guillot (see p. 77) shares his planning process (personal communication, November 6, 2013):

> In order to bring all 150 of my [eighth-grade] students on a quality wetland field experience, I had to develop 6 different stations for them to participate in during the trip. Originally, I looked through all of the science standards to see which fit naturally into this type of setting. Then I designed activities for the outdoor experience that were not possible in the classroom. Over the last few years, in order to give my other teachers more ownership in the trip, I have asked them to create a station for their subject area. This has worked well for social studies (cultural stations to learn about the history and different peoples who have lived here), map skills, math (percentage of land loss in the area), and language arts (poetry). Once we researched the natural and cultural history of the area, it was very easy to create standards-based stations for all of the subjects.

Post-visit Considerations

When Ms. Krings's students got back to the classroom, it was time for play. However, the play was carefully designed to give them time to process what they learned. There were more math problems based on parking meters. There were blocks where students built ramps for cars and a parking garage. Krings reflected that what she heard in their ongoing chatter was the resolution of problems they were working out and the development of important verbal skills.

When Lindsey Halman's (see p. 61) students went to the local woolen mill, they captured images of the place and examined old photos and artifacts. They did a quick write about what they learned when they returned. Their teacher was so impressed with the level of detail and historical understanding that she asked them to spend more time on the project. They used "VoiceThread," a program that combines images and audio and worked in groups to vividly describe the lives of young millworkers and the work they did in the mill. Their "clips" wove in images of the site and the noise of the raging river with the primary sources they examined on-site and the texts they had read beforehand.

Sometimes experiences in the field get lost on return to the classroom. We rush to the next task and assume students will remember the details of the field experience. Take time when you return to the classroom to actively reflect on what was learned. Jigsaw memories, capture images, and plan for where the learning can go. Find ways to keep that connection to the learning that came from the site visit.

> *"The best part doesn't happen at the event. The best part is you get to use it all year long."*

Consider what happens to the questions when you return to the classroom. Discuss with students what is important to know from a visit. What material are they going to be responsible for? In what ways can they apply it to their ongoing work? In naming it, they will be better able to learn it. Make it count.

Ask students to actively share what they learned. What connections are they making? Do they agree with each other? How can they best represent their new learning? Who would benefit from knowing what we learned? If actual data was collected on-site, there are a number of ways to share data online and put data to use. Students can make their findings available to the local community or share globally. Consider what questions remain and how will they direct further research. Mine the experience.

A New View of Literacy

> "Students are complex historical agents and they need to be able to read the multiple texts of their own lives."
>
> *(McLaren, 2003, p. 296)*

In an authentic investigation, the student can see himself as a creator of knowledge, not a passive recipient. When local people, places, and things become sources of new learning in a more fluid pursuit of their own questions, it hints to the learner that he too can be a source of new learning. What he thinks, the breadth of perspectives and the discovery that knowledge might not be a fixed entity illustrates a different way of being and becoming. Learning from these "authentic texts" is fertile ground to ponder: *What is it that I think? What is my opinion? How would I handle this situation?*

Lindsey Halman. Used with permission.

In an afterschool writing program in Tucson, called *Voices: Community Stories Past and Present,* teens gathered to write about their experiences. The stories and photographs generated in this program, that is now part of City High School, were collected and shared as an insert in the local paper. A writing coach reflected on how she encouraged them to write:

> . . . whatever they look like in normal life. [That is] what we're teaching here—that there are stories in the every day. There are stories kind of buried in things that you don't normally think are stories. There are stories in really quiet times. Good journalism doesn't happen only when there are protests and big, big things happening. Good journalism can happen in the quiet everyday life of Tucson, and that's very powerful because most often those stories aren't being told. And so when they're told by people whose voices aren't normally heard—it's doubly powerful.

As mentioned earlier, the Common Core initiatives present an opportunity to better merge the use of printed text and people, places, and things in our communities. We can more effectively consider the ways that learners use text to better weave in the personal, experiential texts of their lives. By pursuing a broader view of literacy, we can expand our view of sources and what is worthwhile for our students to learn about. A new view of literacy can emerge from the current discourse when we pay closer attention to the texts of our students' lives and the places where they live.

COMMON CORE: OPPORTUNITY FOR LOCAL INVESTIGATIONS
READING THE WORLD
The Common Core asks for "increased rigor and complexity" and for learners to explore, analyze, interpret, and excel at communicating their understanding of how the world works. Place-based education invites educators to creatively use the people, places, and artifacts of our local environment alongside traditional texts and investigate the world outside of school as "sites of engagement." Such a practice enriches our view toward the larger purposes of literacy and broadens our vision of what "readiness for life" might look like in our classrooms.
INTEGRATION OF KNOWLEDGE
The Common Core acknowledges the complexity of the learning process and emphasizes the need for connections to rich text. Place-based education affirms the many ways learners' life experiences comes into play as they learn to "read" and "write" and act within the world. Continually, students ask: Is this true given my own experience? Is this true given what I see happening around me? When local experience is woven into traditional, text-based lessons, students have opportunities to become fluent, active, and engaged interpreters of their world and come to learn skills and knowledge as parts of a whole, integrated idea or purpose.
WRITING FOR REAL
The Common Core presents a new emphasis on writing across the curriculum. Place-based education offers a myriad of ways for students to produce authentic, real-world writing for authentic audiences that reflects their new learning. Learning in the context of community presents opportunities for a brochure, website, book, poem, or data bank to serve an authentic purpose. This gives teachers a fresh opportunity to use writing as a tool for understanding, critique, and observation, and for students to produce work in their own voice that is shared with the community for a larger purpose.
NARRATIVES OF OUR PLACES
The Common Core emphasizes the use of informational, non-fiction texts. The view of "place as rich text" gives teachers ways to link printed text to authentic experience and assessment and search for the true, raw, hidden stories of our places. This mix of sources gives us a wider view of literacy as we integrate the insights of young people who search for, write, and read the stories. By coming to understand the stories of our places, students are in a better place to become the authors of their own narratives.
AUTHENTIC RESEARCH
The Common Core identifies the power of research as central to literacy. By aligning curricular tasks with the role of questions, authentic sources of knowledge, and the need for "multiple avenues of exploration," place-based education offers students the opportunity to create authentic questions about the places in which they live. When we incorporate "place as text," we redefine what counts as sources of knowledge and open the way for students to inquire from the people, places, and things that lay waiting in our local communities.

FIGURE 7.2

Amy B. Demarest, Place-based Curriculum Design: Exceeding Standards through Local Investigations. © Routledge, 2015.

> " . . . *A wide spectrum of how . . . out into it you bring your students and you bring the work.* "

Learning to "read the world," as Friere defined it, involves a knowledge that includes action, personal understanding, and a way of being in the world. When students integrate their own learning on this deeper level, their voice becomes critical to the finding and naming of school's purpose. When teachers *engage the local* and students experience the richness of the world outside their classroom, there is space for deep content acquisition and the self-direction of the student. It is not about knowing ahead of time exactly what the student will learn; it is opening up to how a student might set his own course for learning. They might be creating public art, energy-efficient places to live, community websites to barter jobs and materials, or hosting a gathering for elders and second-graders.

"Actitude, not aptitude!"

Learning in this more active way invites new ways to express learning. Knowledge developed in the context of communities is much more colorful. The "rich text" of the real world offers students opportunities to make meaning that is tied into personal questions and the community reality. One educator reflects on this larger purpose:

> My current answer to "why do we have to learn this?" is: So you can learn to read the story for yourselves. If you don't learn how to read the world, then you will be dependent on others to tell you the stories, and you will live your life according to their stories. But learning to read the stories for yourself will allow you to choose your own course.
>
> *(Krapfel, 1999, p. 62)*

Kids become the authors. They write the book. They become the archivists of the community, they collect the data, and they provide the analysis. It is original work. It matters to themselves and the people around them.

★★★★★★★★★★

References

Bailey, L. H. (1909). *The nature-study idea: An interpretation of the new school-movement to put the young into relation and sympathy with nature* (3rd ed. revised). New York, NY: Macmillan.

Bowman Elementary School. (1994). On the path [Unpublished classroom document]. Lexington, MA: Stephen Levy's fourth-grade classroom.

Clark, D. (2008). *Learning to make choices for the future: Connecting public lands, schools, and communities through place-based learning and civic engagement.* Woodstock, VT: The Center for Place-based Learning and Community Engagement.

Cuban, L. (2000). Why is it so hard to get 'good' schools? In L. Cuban & D. Shipps (Eds.), *Reconstructing the common good in education: Coping with intractable American dilemmas* (pp. 148–169). Stanford, CT: State University Press.

Demarest, A. (1997). *This lake alive! An interdisciplinary handbook for teaching and learning about the Lake Champlain Basin.* Shelburne, VT: Shelburne Farms.

Dewey, J. (1938). *Experience and education.* New York, NY: Macmillan.

Friere, P., & Macedo, D. (1987). *Literacy: Reading the word and the world.* Westport, CT: Bergin and Garvey.

Glazer, S. (2004). Community, love and the standards. *Community Works Journal, 6*(3), 8–12.

Guajardo, F. (2007). Teacher, researcher, and agent for community change: A South Texas high school experience. *Journal of Global Initiatives: Policy, Pedagogy, Perspective, 2*(1), 26–42.

Hanson, R. (2004). Giving place a voice. *Community Works Journal, 6*(3), 13–16.

Harvard Graduate School of Education for the Rural Trust (HGSE). (1999). *Living and learning in rural schools and communities: A report to the Annenberg Rural Challenge.* Cambridge, MA: Harvard Graduate School of Education.

Krapfel, P. (1999). Deepening children's participation through ecological investigations. In G. Smith & D. Williams (Eds.), *Ecological education in action: On weaving education, culture, and the environment* (pp. 47–64). Albany: State University of New York Press.

Levy, S. (1996). *Starting from scratch: One classroom builds its own curriculum.* Portsmouth, NH: Heinemann.

Levy, S., & MacGowan, P. (Producers). (1996). *On the path: Tools for an innovative classroom* [DVD]. Burlington, VT: Vanguard Video.

Lusero, L. (2006). How do I get there from Denver: Examining place-based learning at the Logan School. *Democracy and Education, 16,* 57–60.

McLaren, P. (2003). *Life in schools: An introduction to critical pedagogy in the foundations of education* (4th ed.). New York, NY: Allyn and Bacon.

Meier, D. (2003). *In schools we trust: Creating communities of learning in an era of testing and standardization.* Boston, MA: Beacon Press.

Tillman, T. (Ed.). (2007). *Healthy neighborhoods, healthy kids guide* [PDF publication]. Shelburne, VT: Shelburne Farms Sustainable Schools.

Umphrey, M. L. (2007). *The power of community-centered education: Teaching as a craft of place.* Lanham, MD: Rowman & Littlefield.

Wiggins, G., & McTighe, J. (1998). *Understanding by design* (1st ed.). Alexandria, VA: Association for Supervision and Curriculum Development.

Wiggins, G., & McTighe, J. (2005). *Understanding by design* (2nd ed.). Alexandria, VA: Association for Supervision and Curriculum Development.

Wigginton, E. (1985). *Sometimes a shining moment: The foxfire experience.* Garden City, NY: Anchor Press/Doubleday.

Winerip, M. (2012, February 12). A field trip to a strange new place: Second grade visits the parking garage. *The New York Times,* p. A16.

8

PLANNING FOR TEACHING IN LOCAL PLACES

"Oh—I get it!" reflects one teacher. "The field trip IS the lesson!"

The lesson plans, unit outlines, and assessment tasks that comprise teachers' daily lives can be written up as purposeful, artful, and meaningful curriculum. *Understanding by Design* (UbD; Wiggins & McTighe, 1998, 2005), or "planning backwards," offers teachers tools to design curriculum that engages students with the complex task of understanding our world. Because of the clarity of the process, teachers can take big, difficult, complex problems and pose learning opportunities for students that are doable—and measurable. As the backwards design process works, a teacher can then identify what a student would need to know, do, and understand to reach that new learning and then design outcomes and learning activities that will support that journey. When one teacher was asked about planning lessons outside of the classroom, he said: "It's bigger thinking; it's UbD planning." This chapter explores the decisions a teacher makes when grappling with this larger work while using the traditional tools of curriculum design.

The familiar tools we traditionally rely on to document and plan our intentions (lesson plans, unit outlines assessment tools, and outcome expectations) remain the established "currency" of professional development, pre-service licensure, and graduate-level degree programs. The extent to which teachers actually teach from these planning documents varies, but important curriculum decisions take place in their creation. While these products won't change practice, meaningful dialogue about them does. There is power in knowing how to take the larger outcomes that emerge from local investigations and write them up as formal curriculum. In doing so, we become more effective at posing big questions in local places and communicating these larger purposes to others.

"It gets beyond the script."

In this more fluid work, the little tasks are articulated as outcomes alongside the larger accomplishments. Forays deep into the community, explorations in the larger outdoors, hard questions, and unknown answers—these instances of authentic engagement with "place as text" can be our intended purpose. The unexpected, serendipitous questioning becomes the plan.

Having plans doesn't mean that you can't change them. There are many good reasons to change plans. One of your students might have a better idea about what to do, or you may meet up with someone who would be good to stop and listen to. Having a "map" will help you find your way back on the path—or a different route—and get you to your destination. Or the destination may change. You will still know where you are!

The following chart outlines the possible connections of local learning and UbD planning. This chapter is organized on the four sections shown in Figure 8.1.

Essential Questions Happen in Places

> "[P]laces are perceived very differently by different cultural groups who hold different ways of being and knowing. Coming to know a place, therefore means learning the diverse and competing stories told about it. A critical pedagogy of place is concerned not just with the dominant story but with all the stories at risk of being silenced or erased, including the voice of the land itself."
>
> *David Greenwood (2013, pp. 98–99)*

Places are the perfect laboratories to consider big questions. When students come from different neighborhoods and backgrounds, a common understanding of place contributes to building a community of learners. Seeking common ground, exploring sources of food, interlocking systems of energy, and interpreting patterns of human movement can build learners' understanding of the place where they live. A pre-service teacher writes:

> Almost by definition, there is nothing so mundane as "place." Everyone, regardless of race, class, or gender, experiences place. It's the one thing we share in common. It's precisely this commonplaceness which makes place such a valuable springboard for democratic learning.

A view toward *engaging the local* is most simply seen as finding the corollary between an idea and a place. This indeed is an element of learning locally (see Chapter 4), but this view does not cover the intricacies of what happens when students go looking for complex answers in complex places.

For example, it is relatively straightforward to leave the classroom to see how photosynthesis works. Photosynthesis, erosion, flooding, and plant growth all can be observed outside of the classroom. The teacher needs practice to orchestrate this

UNDERSTANDING BY DESIGN AND LOCAL LEARNING

Essential Questions Happen in Places

"Turn the content standards and outcome statements…into question form then design assignments and assessments that evoke possible answers." (UbD, Wiggins & McTighe, 1998, p. 27)

Where else to discover authentic questions and about how the world works but in the places where we live? The forests, streets, streams, fields, and neighborhoods provide the setting for students to explore the BIG IDEAS of literature, social and natural sciences, math, art, and the meaning of civic engagement. These questions, whether subject specific or universal, exist and come to life in the places where we live.

Enduring Understandings Develop in Places

"Evidence of understanding that is transferable involves assessing for students' capacity to use their knowledge thoughtfully and to apply it effectively in diverse settings —that is to do the subject." (UbD, Wiggins & McTighe, 2005, p. 48)

Learning is iterative. Truth-building—for each individual—happens in the context of the places where we live. We come to understand big ideas by engaging in the world around us and verifying or questioning what we already know as we integrate new information. Our communities (natural, built, and human) provide settings to build enduring learning that has been questioned, verified, revisited, and used in collaboration with other people.

Evidence of Authentic Learning Emerges in Places

"As the logic of backwards design reminds us, we are obligated to consider the assessment evidence by the outcomes sought, rather than thinking about assessment primarily as a means for generating grades." (UbD, Wiggins & McTighe, 2005, p. 148)

Places provide an authentic social context for student accomplishment. For students to accomplish worthwhile, meaningful work, they need to do it with and for other people. When students participate in uncovering new information and find an opportunity to share information with and for an authentic audience, they find personal reasons for learning. Authentic assessment is defined when students ask questions and design answers in the context of community and demonstrate mastery of content, process, and lasting and meaningful results.

Teachers Determine Plans for Learning in Places

"How can we take a mass of content knowledge and shape it into engaging, thought-provoking and effective work? (UbD, Wiggins & McTighe, 2005, p. 105)

Designing meaningful learning experiences that align with a clear purpose is a complex and rigorous intellectual activity. With UbD, teachers have a process to take a big idea, frame an essential question, consider what evidence will show this new learning, and then determine a pathway to that understanding. Teachers identify what students need to learn and do and then plan "backwards" to get to that new learning as they engage students in their communities. The actual lesson planning is done in the context of the larger plan.

FIGURE 8.1

Amy B. Demarest, Place-based Curriculum Design: Exceeding Standards through Local Investigations. © Routledge, 2015.

outdoor learning, but it is more manageable when the "idea" is linked to traditional school topics. Questions such as *"What makes leaves green?"* or *"What animals live here?"* or *"When was this built?"* or *"Which direction does the water flow?"* make it easier to track curricular intention and outcome.

However, if you are seeking evidence of climate change or a change in consumer patterns or instances of social justice, it is a much more complicated

enterprise. Traditional school activities do not outline pathways to this complexity. It is not a question of an idea and a place but many ideas in different kinds of places. Teachers and students might be judgmental and think that the stories of some places are "better" than other places. One teacher told me: "My place doesn't have any stories." Perspectives can change. One might see not what is in a place physically—but what happens socially. Students can learn to see beyond the physical attributes of a place to see how the parts interact and explore the systems that govern places rather than single events.

> "Gardens are not just a little break from the endless, mindless stretch of pavement; they become gathering places, sanctuaries, cultural and social centers . . . as important to the health of our civic life as are art museums, theaters and great restaurants. They are part of a city's soul."
> Michael Ableman (quoted in Stone, 2009, p. 23)

Some questions can be explored in all places. Community, diversity, and change over time and systems are large concepts that can illuminate the inner workings of a place. A large question such as *How does this place work?* can be applied to different environments. Students can experience ways to interpret different places with a familiar lens. *Is this place safe? How have humans impacted this environment? How do people get their food?* These are universal questions.

In planning, the teacher needs to consider what big ideas can be learned in what places. The process of identifying "Big Ideas" and "Learning Opportunities" helps guide the process. The chart "What Kinds of Places" (see Figure 8.2) suggests some different possibilities. While urban areas offer a multitude of lessons about living together and are windows to global questions of sustainability and diversity, they can also be sites to explore natural systems and interdependence. Some places suggest certain questions to the exclusion of others. We would tend to look in natural places for instances of plant succession and erosion, rural places for stories of old buildings and farming, and urban places for traffic issues, high-rise dwellings, and changing demographics. However, in this ever-changing world, we lessen our opportunities by limiting certain lessons to certain places.

With a deeper and more fluid view of what our places can teach us, we can consider nesting structures in a city environment and social gathering places in the forest. We can understand more about plants as they thrive in urban centers, and we can examine diverse meanings of community in all places. We can continually rethink what lessons are offered by our large, troubled, complex, and wondrous world.

I remember visiting the historic site in Concord, Massachusetts, where the American Revolution started in 1776. There was a wooden bridge that led to the field where the "shot heard round the world" was fired, but my attention stopped

WHAT KINDS OF PLACES?	
NATURAL AREAS	
Topics and Big Ideas	**Learning Opportunity**
Plant succession and function, food chains interdependence, relationships	Explore site and have students capture digital images of instances of interdependence. Create a storybook of interrelationships.
Bio-diversity	Gather a local bio-index of living things—examine patterns of species and compare local place to other places—worldwide
Climate disruption	Data collection and interpretation; compare local to global phenomenon, share data globally (Project Bud-Burst).
RURAL AREAS	
Topics and Big Ideas	**Learning Opportunity**
Old barns; relics of the past (jobs, land, water)	Explore stories of courage that old buildings can tell. Create photo story of site; enter stories on Google Maps. Compile architectural drawings of traditional designs.
Change over time	Map development over time; identify segments of history. Overlay different development patterns.
Land use: How do the people in our town use the land?	Collect and share visions of the future. Conduct mathematical spatial analysis of land use. Presentation to town government and post on local website.
URBAN AREAS	
Topics and Big Ideas	**Learning Opportunity**
What is a city? Urban issues—near and far	Map human services; develop criteria for quality of life. Compare ancient city: what are gathering places, sources of food, laws, dress, customs?
Infrastructure: What holds this place together?	Create narrated videos of systems that support built structures. Artifact interpretation: What does this thing do?
Diversity: What are the hidden stories in our community?	Ethnographic study of different cultures—interviews, murals, maps to show layers of history and changing demographics. Create signage in different languages or different images.
SUBURBAN AREAS	
Topics and Big Ideas	**Learning Opportunity**
Patterns in the landscape	Map geometric patterns of buildings and development. Where do they work? How far is their commute?
How do people get what they need?	Map traffic patterns and transportation of goods and services.
Where will our last green space be?	Create inventory of green space/sustainable development.

FIGURE 8.2

Amy B. Demarest, Place-based Curriculum Design: Exceeding Standards through Local Investigations. © Routledge, 2015.

at the foot bridge that spanned a swampy area on the edge of the woods. I had just recently finished a course in wetland ecology, and I was seeing swamps with new eyes. I spent most of our visit leaning over the bridge to watch the algae and creatures swimming around, the plants growing in the shallow water, and the mysterious bubbles rising from the muck. While my family went on to investigate one story, I stopped at another.

You cannot always plan what story students will experience. We might want students to explore nature only to discover that natural places do not seem safe and fun to all learners. Or we may overlook, with the best of intentions, what one place might mean to a student. Consider if a teacher wants to bring students to a food pantry to educate them about the homeless and fails to take into account that some of her students might be clients. Places have many stories, some of which may be hidden to us when we start our investigations.

Selwyn (2010) poses the connections between "hidden history" and places where "clues to who we are and how we got that way reside in the work that we do, [and] the ways that we live in the world . . . " (p. 142). He goes on to say:

There is significant history in the buildings and structures of any place, of any environment. There is obvious information conveyed by the kinds of land plots, dwellings and structures, the materials from which they are constructed, the slopes and angles of the roofs, the design and shape of their building footprints and the length of time they are designed to last. . . . But there are other stories told by the buildings and structures, more complex stories about who has lived in a place and how they have lived. Many of these stories are told most eloquently by those buildings that have been abandoned. Virtually every town or city in our age . . . features large abandoned factories, often surrounded by chain-link fences, themselves rusted and compromised by time and weather. We walk, bike, bus or drive past them on a daily basis, perhaps giving them a moment's notice but rarely two as we continue to our destination, which they no longer are.

(pp. 143–144).

Enduring Understandings Develop in Places

"The search for meaning takes a different route for each student. Even when educators structure classroom lessons and curriculum to ensure that all students learn the same concepts at the same time, each student still constructs his or her own unique meaning through his or her own cognitive processes."

Jacqueline Brooks & Martin Brooks (1999, p. 21)

Teachers often express their desire to foster their students' personal connection to the places where they live. Learning the history, the ecology, and the story of a place brings students into closer contact with how the world works. Many teachers believe that taking care of a place emerges from this personal connection. A teacher might consider what information her students can learn about a place and what personal meaning it will generate. Thus, one student may become vested in the community through ecological caretaking while another may gain an entrepreneurial advantage. Such openness to the many stories of our places gives students the opportunity to see their place anew and determine its own relevance.

Directly addressing how youth view their communities can tap into an "inner script" related to how they perceive options in the place where they live. A young person's "script" might run something like this: "*I live in a dump where nothing ever happens and nothing ever will. . . .*" This perspective might be challenged by a new storyline: "*I live in a place that is economically depressed now because of the auto industry. These old buildings tell a story of a vibrant past—and although that is not happening now, it doesn't mean that it can't happen here again.*" A young person who thinks, "*Nothing ever happens here!*" may feel differently after getting to know some neighbors while tackling a community issue. The "happening" may be a new feeling that comes from friendship, work, play, and dialogue.

Julia Putnam (2011) reflects on being invited as a teenager to take part in Detroit Summer in 1992—one of the first signs of widespread renewal in Detroit.

> I was one of the kids who knew how to "do" school. But I was miserable. I lived in a city that everyone described as a crumbling cesspool, and I could not understand why this was so. I also did not understand what I should do about it. The answer presented to me was unsatisfying—get good grades, go to college, and get a high-paying job so I could leave Detroit and all of its problems behind for someone else.
>
> One day . . . my friend [gave me] a flyer [about] Detroit Summer . . . [that said] in every significant social movement in our country, young people had been the defining factor. They needed people who were willing to take on the challenge of revitalizing, redefining and respiriting Detroit from the ground up. I had not even known that I craved being asked to do something important until I was actually asked.
>
> *(p. 58)*

For Putnam, being invited into the possibility of making her community a better place totally altered how she felt about where she lived—but more importantly about her own life. What was making her "miserable" wasn't alleviated by more academic knowledge but by a deeper, more critical view of the place where she lived. This complex mix of feelings, abilities, intellect, and one's sense of personal future all contribute to how a student experiences school.

"I want my students to learn to love this place and feel a sense of belonging."

Teachers can tackle the emotional aspect of their teaching more directly. Two sixth-grade teachers in Vermont talked about how they wanted their students to experience the joy of gardening. As they designed their unit on food, they considered how they might foster a "sense of joy." They asked how students might receive useful feedback on their growing ability to enjoy working outdoors. How might they more intentionally celebrate this satisfaction of working in the soil? They decide to talk more about it with their students and put it on the rubric. They figured out how to be more transparent in their intentions and were open to the student who does not "love to garden" or may have had no previous experience working outside.

"I'm really into insects. Do you think I could do something with insects out here?"

Elliott Lax, a teacher who taught at City High School in Tucson, Arizona, worked with students in a community garden on the outskirts of the city. Service is an integral part of the school curriculum and the school partners with local organizations to address food equity in Tucson. When I asked him why students would participate in the community garden, he described the many different reasons:

> I think it would depend on the kid and how much understanding and ownership they have. Some might say, "I'm working down here because this garden belongs to the school . . . we're going to be doing projects here forever." Someone else might say, "I'm down here because I want to learn about gardening and food production and food issues for Tucson." Or, "I was looking for a class where I got to do a lot of manual labor and I really like getting hot, smelly, sticky." Or a kid might say, "You know I really don't like gardening and this class isn't really what I imagined. But I like the fact that we're making signs and we get to paint them and the garden is something that we're proud of."

Elliot marveled the many ways students relate to the garden experience and saw his job as figuring out how to accommodate those different pathways. "The hard part," he says, "is . . . making everybody feel like they have a role to play and . . . take pride and ownership [in it] . . . whatever the project is and to recognize that everybody's angle on it is going to be slightly different."

A teacher might name a "sense of place" as part of her formal feedback system and invite students to consider how to express their feelings about where they live. An assessment tool such as the one below might help the student develop a deeper understanding through an ecological, historical, or an artistic lens. The teacher would still identify it and provide performance descriptions to communicate her intentions. A teacher might consider the criteria shown in Figure 8.3.

ASSESSMENT TOOL: SENSE OF PLACE	
CRITERIA:	**PERFORMANCE DESCRIPTION:**
SENSE OF PLACE	• Expresses personal feelings about place. • Volunteers new learning and is able to share and discuss with peers and community partners. • Makes connections to ways that another (writer, poet, artist) has expressed feelings about a place. • Applies specific skills appropriate to the task. • Seeks ways to protect place. • Offers multiple interpretations of how people over time have interacted with the environment.

FIGURE 8.3

Amy B. Demarest, Place-based Curriculum Design: Exceeding Standards through Local Investigations.
© Routledge, 2015.

Facets of Understanding

The Facets of Understanding, as defined by Wiggins and McTighe (2005), underline the complexity of a student's pathway to understanding. They say it is like a prism, "a family of interrelated abilities" (p. 4), not a linear progression. Exploring

LOCAL FACETS OF UNDERSTANDING
EXPLAIN...provide through supported and justifiable accounts of phenomena, facts, and data.
What are the characteristics of this region? Who lives here? What is the habitat like? What is the work that people do here? What are the customs and ethnic heritage? Where do people live, and how do they get around? How have the features of this place changed over time? What is the quality of this water?
INTERPRETATION...tell meaningful stories, offer apt representations with personal dimension, use of images, anecdotes, analogies, and models.
What is meaningful about this place? What does this place say about who we are? How have different groups of people related to this place? What story can this landscape tell: the rocks, the fences, the vegetation, and so forth? How have humans impacted this landscape? How can I artistically represent my understanding of this place?
APPLICATION...ability to usefully and appropriately use knowledge in new and diverse contexts.
What is needed to solve this problem? What is a good management practice for this place? How should this place be protected? How should this building be protected? What should people know about this place in order to care for it? How can I change my actions to better match my convictions? Who can I bring together to help address this issue? Does this graph represent this change accurately? Who will find this information helpful?
PERSPECTIVE...to provide critical and insightful points of view from different vantage points.
How do other people value this place? How do people's sense of place affect what happens here? In what ways do living things depend on the same land and water that I do? What are the different points of view I see in my local government, neighborhood, school community? How can I better understand the diversity of my community? What makes this person behave this way? What conflicts come about from different people's perspectives?
EMPATHY...to get inside another person's feelings, find value in what others might consider odd or alien.
What would it feel like if...? Why does this person act like that? How can I make our classroom a more comfortable, safer place to learn? What must I understand about this person before we work together on a service project? How did the author/artist/activist feel about this place? How can I help this person learn something new about this place?
SELF-KNOWLEDGE...the wisdom to know one's ignorance, abilities, and patterns of thought and action. Ability to identify and direct deeper learning.
What is my connection to this place? What will I do to protect it? What is my impact/footprint in this place? What skills or special talents can I bring to this project? How does my attitude affect my actions and this place? What possibilities are there for me here? What are my prejudices or pre-conceived opinions against this group of people? What talents can I bring to this undertaking? What weaknesses do I want to be aware of as I enter this community partnership? How can I make this team more effective? What else should I know before I start?

FIGURE 8.4

Amy B. Demarest, Place-based Curriculum Design: Exceeding Standards through Local Investigations. © Routledge, 2015.

the facets can illuminate the many ways students come to answer questions in local places. Teachers use this prism like a checklist when planning units to broaden their thinking. This is not to imply that all facets are supposed to be addressed in one study, but they provide a way for teachers to better understand how their students learn. Teachers often see a new dimension to a lesson they are planning that they hadn't considered.

In *Teaching History with Museums*, Marcus, Stoddard, and Woodward (2012) maintain that students can develop "historical empathy" when they meet up with artifacts from the past and that this is key to developing an understanding of the past. The object itself can be instructive in drawing the students into the narrative of history. In their view, museums offer many opportunities for a deeper, more critical interpretation:

> Students can evaluate which artifacts museums use, how they use artifacts to tell a selective story about the past, and how representations of culture and collective memory or post-memory are constructed through exhibits . . . They can also compare the stories and historical narratives from museums with those found in their textbooks or other historical sources.
>
> *(p. 13)*

Such a view invites much more engagement with artifacts. Armed with a better understanding of the facets, teachers can be more intentional about planning a museum visit or any field experience. Teachers find themselves saying: "Oh yes, they are really learning to interpret here; not just explain" or "What I am asking for really is self-knowledge, to be able to learn that about themselves. I should be clearer about that." Or "There is an opportunity to develop perspective in this project; that is what they are really doing. I need to pay more attention to that." By "paying attention," a teacher might discuss it more openly with their students, ask them to actively reflect on different perspectives, and include it as assessment criteria for a final project.

"It's not just about the murals. Our teacher has us explore our personal dreams."

Teachers learn to track understanding when they see its many dimensions. For example, a teacher who asks her students to be involved in a mural project that expresses the community heritage of a neighborhood might include empathy as part of the process. Being able to articulate and strive for this objective facilitates the learning and encourages the student to pay attention. If empathy is a stated goal, a teacher would need to create time for students to understand another's viewpoint and to discuss strategies for incorporating different experiences. The project isn't just about getting the mural done; it's about human interaction and expression. The teacher could foster ways for both the students and community participants to give feedback on how they felt during the process and what they learned about different perspectives. Pauline Roberts (see p. 89) (personal communication, October 23, 2013) shares a reflection that shows the new perspective and self-knowledge gained by a student who worked to educate others about sustainability:

> From doing this project, I have learned that I am very persistent. I know what I want, and if people don't listen and [they] say no, I will keep on talking until they say yes or see my point. I get kind of annoyed if people don't give me their full attention, or if they just don't seem interested. I will keep on bugging them about it. It may be kind of annoying, but as long as people know about the important things I am trying to tell them about, it's OK.

Curricular tools and time for reflection support this self-awareness. A rubric might assess artistic expression, quality of artistic medium, expression of multiple experiences, and a feeling of confidence. During and following the project, all participants might have time to reflect on how inclusive the process was by answering questions such as: *"In what ways do I feel listened to?"* or *"In what ways was I better able to listen to others?"* and *"How did this project help me express a human experience different than my own?"* The facets of understanding give teachers an opportunity to name the complexity of local investigations.

Evidence of Authentic Learning Emerges in Places

> "The school must open its doors. It must reach out to spread itself, and come into direct contact with all its people. Each day the power of the school must be felt in some corner of the school district. It must work so that everybody sees its work and daily appreciates its work."
>
> *Angelo Patri (1917, p. 213)*

Wiggins and McTighe (2005) have invited us to make classrooms "courtrooms" where we seek evidence to prove students "guilty of understanding" (p. 148). Consider what happens when the "evidence" for a guilty verdict develops in the larger community. When students are doing the work outside of school and interacting with the people in the community, the evidence becomes public. It is shared with many different people. New expressions of excellence emerge.

While the UbD model provides numerous insights into all of the assessment process, two aspects of this approach are particularly relevant to place-based education:

- the identification of the embedded knowledge and skills, and
- consideration of how to assess content, process and result.

Identifying Knowledge and Skills

A critical skill teachers need in order to give feedback on authentic tasks is the ability to identify the knowledge and skills embedded in standard-based investigations. As the teacher unpacks a standard, she will consider what knowledge and skills a student should learn in order to understand (this complex idea). The unit is organized around giving students time to practice the new knowledge and skills in a variety of ways. They are the building blocks to the enduring understanding and need to be taught and assessed intentionally. They are parts to the whole.

The knowledge and skills gained are learned for a reason. They are not delivered and processed in isolation but gain meaning as students become stewards of the land, visit protected areas, examine old pipes, map out threatened spaces, and peruse land use maps. The essential question fuels the learning. Wiggins and McTighe (2005) state that "the ability to transfer our knowledge and skills effectively involves the capacity to take what we know and use it creatively, flexibly, fluently, in different settings or problems, on our own" (p. 40).

If a student becomes inspired by the story of an old building or a creek behind the shopping mall, he may not realize that he is also learning how to map, interview, record, analyze, classify, and so forth. Being able to clearly identify the elements of understanding help the teacher and student track the learning and better communicate about its progress. A teacher who wants her students to build a connection to place might identify the specific knowledge and skills shown in Figure 8.5.

ESSENTIAL QUESTION: WHAT IS MY PERSONAL CONNECTION TO THIS PLACE, AND WHAT DO I MOST WANT TO PROTECT?
ENDURING UNDERSTANDING: People are connected to their place in a variety of ways and are inspired to protect their place for different reasons.
KNOW: Students will gain new KNOWLEDGE of:
Specific plants, animals, biodiversity of region, cultural history, cultural eras and the technological changes that defined each era, the geology "story" of change over time, oral traditions, ancient and modern stories about values and human behavior, environmental threats to region, economic hardships, artistic expression of place, how other humans protect this place, and one's personal impact or "eco-footprint."
DO: Students will gain the ABILITY to:
Map out region to record different stories, identify and interpret threats to region, identify landforms, classify plants and animals, interpret "stories" in the landscape, express feelings about place in writing and through a chosen form of artistic expression, conduct research about place including interviews, and present plan on preservation-conservation and/or sustainable practice.

FIGURE 8.5

Amy B. Demarest, Place-based Curriculum Design: Exceeding Standards through Local Investigations. © Routledge, 2015.

Content, Process, Result

Another useful UbD nugget is the advice to more clearly distinguish what we are assessing. Wiggins and McTighe (2005) point out the need to clearly communicate performance criteria and have distinguished between *content, process,* and *result.* Identifying these elements inform the assessment process and suggest these questions for the teacher to consider:

*   What *content* knowledge will a student need to know?
*   What *process* will they use to learn new material and express their findings?
*   What is the *result* of this work?

Considering these three aspects of assessment separately helps us give better feedback and adds clarity to the design process. Instead of the all-too-familiar "Great effort!" and "Good job!" that we so easily bestow, a student needs more pertinent feedback to improve the work. We more readily say, "This math equation is correct" than "I appreciate the tenacity you showed us when you were faced with that difficult situation." It is easier to give feedback on this more personal trait if there has been a discussion of tenacity—or what one teacher calls "stick-to-it-ness." When students and teachers recognize together what they are striving for, the task of going forward has more traction.

Content seems to be the most straightforward of things to assess. The teacher might track if the student knows certain information on a test or a written essay. However, in complex tasks, the content is often more challenging to assess. In working with teachers to design better assessment tools, there is often a realization that the elements of the task need to be broken apart more carefully. Instead of asking for "demonstration of scientific understanding," it is more useful to ask for more concrete examples of "how living organisms interact" or "ways humans impact water systems." If looking for evidence of a student understanding "change over time," language such as "provides example of physical changes" or "illustrates detailed and accurate 'before and after' image" is useful. When teachers analyze the task, they learn to be more intentional about adding content-based criteria that provides a cleaner handle for the student.

Teachers are more adept at assessing process. Teachers might clearly outline and assess the writing process, appropriate use of technology, or the ability to participate in group work. Teachers can also identify traits that support a specific process. If group work is a focus, it is more productive to identify when a student is "actively listening" or "supports the suggestions of others." This also makes peer assessment much more effective and easier to organize.

A teacher might say: "It was helpful to talk about my assessment tool. I thought I was assessing the science because my students made these amazing models and I knew they knew it—but the tool gave them feedback on the process and whether they had organized the material and expressed it clearly. That is important but I needed to be clearer about the content. Where is the evidence they knew the science?"

The deeper result of a student's work is not often assessed. We refer to the result in a narrow way in the context of outcomes-based assessment (i.e., Did they get the answer right? Was it a good result? Did they master this concept?). Wiggins (personal communication, 2013) encourages us to go further: "OK, that's the content. Now what do you want them to be able to do with it, on their own, in the future?"

Authentic investigations prompt us to think about the lasting impact of the student work. *What difference does it make? Did anything change as a result of this work?* In an earlier conversation with Wiggins (personal communication, 2000), he prompted me to think of the result in a new way. Does the question have a lasting impact on the thinking of the learner or others who have shared in the investigations? With this wider view of result, a teacher might assess specific criteria such as the ability to "prompt a new behavior" or "express a new perspective."

When teachers seek to integrate democratic action into the work they assign, it becomes even more important to consider its impact. *Does it matter to oneself? To others?* When students design playgrounds, visit elders, build housing, cook meals, and create powerful community art, the results generate a new feeling in the community. A teacher will still consider questions such as "Do they get the vocabulary in this section?" but also others such as "What action will this learning inspire?"

Berger (1991) believes in the power of critique and likens the tools of good reflection and assessment to those of a surgeon who must be concise in his or her work. He sees this precision as the key to building common understanding of what is excellent work. While studying architecture with his students, his class hosted a number of visits from practicing architects who shared the language of their craft. He describes that "without the concepts and technical language we learned from these practitioners, we never could have viewed and critiqued our own design efforts capably" (p. 36). Community partners and internships become critical in the assessment process by providing this "real-world context" to the work.

In a clear assessment plan the teacher will determine what evidence will illustrate new learning. Specific products and performances provide opportunity for formative feedback. In assessing the quality of an outcome, a teacher will assess content, process, and result. In thinking about a summative assessment to the question, "What is my personal connection to this place and what do I most want to protect?" a student might demonstrate the ability to:

- explain the many stories and biodiversity of region (content),
- express feeling about a place (result),
- apply content-knowledge (discipline-specific vocabulary, interpretation, and information) to a narrative (i.e., geology, history, ethnic, biology, soil . . .) (content),
- plan and conduct research and share original findings (process),

- use technology for own purposes (process), and
- convince others of a point of view (result).

Throughout the unit, students learn and practice different ways to demonstrate their increasing mastery of the criteria and receive ongoing, formative feedback. A culminating activity that embraces all of these elements becomes a "container" that merges specific knowledge and skills with a student's "final" response to the essential question.

The result of a student's work is more authentic when there is time for it to be shared and processed by others. It may be a small writing conference, videoconferencing, or a town meeting. Oftentimes, final reflections the day after the celebrations are fruitful. The "final" work can generate new understandings. Structuring reflection time, planning, goal setting, and action planning can all be part of the "end" of a unit.

Kathleen Maas-Hebner, Oregon State University. Used with permission.

Teachers Determine Plans for Learning in Places

> "Teachers must become the creators of curriculum rather than the dispensers of curriculum developed by others [and] become able to make the link between the unpredictable activities that can happen beyond the classroom and student performance standards set by the district or state."
>
> *Greg Smith (2002, p. 593)*

There are two kinds of products teachers create in the planning process: lesson planning and unit planning. Lesson planning is for designing single instances of focused learning that addresses part of the unit standards, whereas unit planning is designed for ongoing exploration of an essential question.

When designing a place-based unit, the teacher considers what local places might be part of the overall plan. A teacher working with the Essential Question,

How has this place changed over time? might decide that one of the unit standards is the Next Generation Science Standards (NGSS, 2013) "Stability and Change" cross-cutting concept: "Stability and change are ways of describing how a system functions. Whether studying ecosystems or engineered systems, the question is often to determine how the system is changing over time, and which factors are causing the system to become unstable" (p. 12).

She might also consider the National Council for the Social Studies (NCSS) Social Studies Standards (NCSS, 2013) that include "Change, Continuity, and Context," a standard that ". . . means assessing similarities and differences between historical periods and between the past and present. It also involves coming to understand how a change in one area of life relates to a change in other areas, thus bringing together political, economic, intellectual, social, cultural, and other factors" (p. 46). From these big ideas, she would determine what knowledge and skills were important to address in specific lessons. For example, from reading these standards carefully, she may determine that the *ability to identify factors that have altered an aspect of a system* or *the ability to compare and contrast two historical periods or compare changes in two areas of life* were things her students should know.

She might design a number of different lessons that prompt her students to see the different ways change happens. Some might be site-based while others involve background research in the classroom. One site-based lesson might explore natural changes such as flooding and vegetation while another might investigate human-made changes such as jobs, transportation, or energy use. She might explore whether it is correct to distinguish between human and "naturally" made changes. Toward the end of a unit, the teacher might ask her students to identify other sites that illustrate a different kind of change: soil erosion, new buildings, new highways, and the way landscapes have changed from farms to condominiums or the way cityscapes have changed from factories to deserted lots . . . to farmland again! Scaffolding gives students an opportunity to understand these changes from different perspectives—and most importantly their own.

Unit design reflects one kind of planning, being able to think with the big idea, considering what evidence would show enduring understanding, and designing a sequence of learning activities that builds understanding alongside the development of specific knowledge and skills. Having done this larger thinking, the teacher then proceeds to design individual lessons, some of which might take place outside of the classroom.

While planning a specific site-based lesson, the challenge is to be intentional about what students will learn from a specific place. The learning—as explored in Chapter 7—might be more multi-dimensional and challenging. We can get them on the bus or walk outside the door, but to actually structure meaningful learning in specific places is hard. A teacher will ask: "What will we actually do at the market, by the shore, at the factory, on the sidewalk, or in the field (literally)? What aspect of this place do I want them to really grapple with?"

One of the ways that I try to frame this kind of thinking is to tweak the structure of a traditional lesson plan to accommodate a more intentional plan for learning in places. This adjustment includes thinking about how the site visit integrates into your larger plan and identifying what your students will learn before, at, and after the site visit (see Figure 7.1).

The "Sites of Engagement" template (see Figure 8.6) is slightly different than a traditional learning plan. Like any good standards-based lesson, a piece of a standard or a smaller cluster of standards is addressed, not the whole thing, although

---

"SITES OF ENGAGEMENT" LESSON PLAN

What is the CONTEXT of this learning experience?
Include the ESSENTIAL QUESTION/if applicable.

Is there a larger outcome and longer plan of which this is a part? What is the unit plan? What standards does this unit address, and what part of the standards is the focus of this lesson? What have students learned or experienced prior to this lesson that is important to note?

WHERE will this "engagement" take place?

Decide on a place to engage students in a learning experience. What is it about this place that illuminates an aspect of your essential question?

What is the PLAN for your students?

Create a "lesson plan" for the learning experience. Include what students will do before they go, what they will do on-site, and what they will do after they return to the classroom. Note: This can be over a number of days or within one or two class periods.

Pre-visit:

On-site:

Post-visit:

What is the OUTCOME of this experience?

Create a student handout (or specific directions) that describes the work that students will do (a product such as a nature journal, inventory of patterns, or performance such as a skit or song). Include how this outcome will be assessed with specific criteria.

What resources/preparation are needed for you to be ready for this experience?
In what ways does this plan incorporate other district/grade-level expectations?

FIGURE 8.6

Amy B. Demarest, Place-based Curriculum Design: Exceeding Standards through Local Investigations. © Routledge, 2015.

the relevance of the part to the whole is constantly kept in view. The trick is for students to rigorously interrogate some aspect of the site and be able to interpret, observe, and engage with some characteristic of the place. They also need time to make some sense of that encounter and to express that learning in some tangible way.

Teachers might consider a particular aspect of a place such as weathering patterns, flooding or other threats to riparian habitats, evidence of a community gathering place, an infrastructure puzzle or swamp, changes in transportation, or a way that an old building contrasts to newer developments. As we have seen in so many ways illustrated in this book, different places have different stories. The elements of the template invite the considerations presented in Figure 8.6.

★★★★★★★★★★

The foundation of place-based curriculum design is when teachers and students together develop questions that emerge from local places and generate findings that are specific, clear, and measurable. As teachers rethink the actual products that students create, student work is transformed. Rather than filling out worksheets, students are writing books and filing reports; their work is original and important to others around them.

Although all the elements of local learning might not be fully developed in one teacher's plan, the potential for all of these aspects of learning to be affected is ongoing. When teachers *engage the local,* they find ways to make students' real lives and the places they live part of the everyday life of the schoolhouse. A student's experience, content knowledge, sense of place, and future possibilities can all resonate when local investigations are underway. Teachers take outcomes such as talking in front of local officials or growing food for their neighbors and develop criteria, structure research, and create assessment tools that help students work toward excellence. Moments of democracy and civic engagement are woven into lesson plans, outcomes, and focusing questions.

★★★★★★★★★★

References

Berger, R. (1991). Building a school culture of high standards: A teacher's perspective. In V. Perrone (Ed.), *Expanding student assessment* (pp. 32–39). Alexandria, VA: Association for Supervision and Curriculum Development.

Brooks, M. G., & Brooks, J. G. (1999). The courage to be constructivist. *Educational Leadership 57*(3), 18–24.

Greenwood, D. (2013). A critical theory of place-conscious education. In R. B. Stevenson, M. Brody, J. Dillon, & A. E. J. Wals (Eds.), *International handbook on environmental education* (pp. 93–100). New York, NY: Routledge.

Marcus, A. S., Stoddard, J. D., & Woodward, W. W. (2012). *Teaching history with museums: Strategies for K-12 social studies.* New York, NY: Routledge.

National Council for the Social Studies (NCSS). (2013). *The college, career, and civic life (C3) framework for social studies state standards: Guidance for enhancing the rigor of K-12 civics, economics, geography, and history*. Silver Spring, MD: NCSS.

Next Generation Science Standards (NGSS). (2013, April). NGSS release. Retrieved on August 6, 2014, from www.nextgenscience.org/sites/ngss/files/Appendix%20G%20-%20Crosscutting%20Concepts%20FINAL%20edited%204.10.13.pdf

Patri, A. (1917). *A schoolmaster of the great city*. New York, NY: Macmillan.

Putnam, J. P. (2011). Another education is happening. *Monthly Review, 63*(3), 56–63.

Selwyn, D. (2010). *Following the threads: Bringing inquiry research into the classroom*. New York, NY: Peter Lang.

Smith, G. (2002). Place-based education: Learning to be where we are. *Phi Delta Kappan, 83*(8), 584–594.

Stone, M. K. (2009). *Smart by nature: Schooling for sustainability*. Healdsburg, CA: Watershed Media.

Wiggins, G., & McTighe, J. (1998). *Understanding by design* (1st ed.). Alexandria, VA: Association for Supervision and Curriculum Development.

Wiggins, G., & McTighe, J. (2005). *Understanding by design* (2nd ed.). Alexandria, VA: Association for Supervision and Curriculum Development.

PART IV

Moving Forward

Strategies for School Change

These days, a teacher's creative capacity is thwarted by the many prescriptive tasks that shape her time with students. The weight of high-stakes testing restricts what is learned and how it is taught. These intrusions not only hinder the energy necessary to teach and learn, but are an unprecedented constraint on the freedom it takes to become a better teacher. Working autonomously and practicing their art become acts of democracy for teachers. New insights provide fresh pathways toward a sounder practice. While these insights are the wellsprings of good teaching, they are seldom the inspiration behind the menu of professional development efforts designed to "improve" teaching. In order for schools to really change, we need a better understanding of learning—an understanding that underlines the collaborative, social, and participatory nature of knowledge—for teachers and students.

Coming to see learning as collaborative inquiry informs our view of the power of place- and community-based education. Teachers need not be isolated in their classrooms with their students but can instead forge meaningful associations with other "teachers" outside of school—the people, places, and perplexities of the places where we live. The work generated from local investigations is not confined to classrooms; it is shared with others in the community. Teachers can collaborate in supportive and fruitful ways to integrate content and address real community needs. These relationships become a refreshing and renewable source of inspiration, affirmation, and possibility.

This is why place-based education is often referred to as a school change movement. Its agenda challenges the assumptions about what students should do each day and the structure that holds those practices in place. While there are many best practices that emerge as recognizable markers in this approach, it is a more personal journey than learning "how-to" do something. It is fundamentally a movement toward a new way of teaching—a larger possibility. When teachers make these changes, a synergy develops between the teacher, learner, and the community that fills the school with a sense of forward motion.

One teacher's "spark" might be different than another's. One teacher might be triggered by a realization that a trip to a meadow can be a finely orchestrated science lab, while another might learn how to incorporate reflection with community service and see how much more it means to students. A teacher might be impressed at the depth of a student's presentation on alternative energy or marvel at a student's artistic expression of community treasures. Another teacher might see a group of students present to a town council and say, "Wow, I want my students to have an experience like that."

This forward movement, in whatever form, is what happens when teachers undertake local investigations. There is no "done." There is no "got it." Teachers and students create forward motion toward a new way of doing school that alters the ecology of the schoolhouse. In the doing, they build an energy that emerges from the nature, reality, dilemmas, and possibilities of the places where they live. It sometimes resembles school transformation, it sometimes is a teacher's personal quest for meaning or a school-wide effort to increase academic rigor. Whatever the entry point, whatever the process, whatever the outcome, it energizes teachers with a refreshed view of their ability to create better schools for young people.

TEACHER PORTRAIT #7
ANNE TEWKSBURY-FRYE
ELEMENTARY

"Who are we as individuals and who are we as a community?"

There was a pouring rain the spring evening Anne's fourth- and fifth-grade students displayed their photographs of the neighborhood. On the stairs, the photos were clustered on the wall, mounted with masking tape, with the photographer's name and photo title in silver ink on a black paper frame—titles such as "Me and My Sister," "Recess Is Over," "My Family," and "This Is My Street." The pictures were taken under the tutelage of a high school student intern who approached Anne about doing a photography project with her class.

On the long hallway, each child had chosen one best photo to have mounted formally with captions. There was a mix of guests: families, the high school student's teacher, her family and friends, three school-board members, the principal and her family, Anne's husband, and other friends of the school. The rain poured on the metal rooftop, the sound not enough to hamper the warm fellowship inside.

Anne is all heart and purpose. Her classroom is the world. The school she teaches in sits in the middle of a changing and sometimes troubled neighborhood. Amid snippets of many languages, Anne moves around the room so fast, making so many decisions at once it can make your head spin. Her comments sound like a how-to catalogue of differentiated instruction as she touches base with each student: "I love the way you put your name on the paper first." ". . . Stretch your mind a little more," she whispers to one student on her way to give directions at the front of the room.

A "kindness curriculum" came about because "there was a wound in the classroom. So we just dropped everything and said: this is what we have to do." Each student decorated a journal titled, "Friends around the Classroom, around the World." They take time daily to think about acts of kindness they had witnessed and taken part in. They answer the question, "What were the times that you saw the kindness?" and a question she asks a lot, "What does that mean to you?" Her students' mastery of English is so varied that it challenges her to hit a wide range in a short time—like an opera singer's startling range of song. She helps a student spell the sentence, "He is helping me"; reads another's passage and comments, "That is so wise"; and says to another, "I love that sentence."

At year's end, her students listed the things they had done to help others. The long list included cleaning up the neighborhood and raising money for the food shelf, a holiday party for the homeless, and contributions to victims of Katrina. When I asked her students if someone gave them only one week to learn the most important thing, what should they do first? They answered a mix of reading, writing, math, how to make a difference, help the environment, and compost. One student summed it up: " . . . you can learn how to help your neighborhood and learn to write at the same time."

9

CHANGING PRACTICE CHANGES SCHOOLS

"And if we do act, in however small a way, we don't have to wait for some grand utopian future. The future is an infinite succession of presents, and to live now as we think human beings should live, in defiance of all that is bad around us, is itself a marvelous victory."

Howard Zinn (2006, p. 170)

Changes in practice often come from moments when teachers come to see their work—and the work that students do—differently. These "moments" change a teacher's view of what might be possible, which, in turn, fuel further change. When a teacher makes sense of the tangle of relationships and directives that shape the school day, new ways of teaching become apparent. Such changes do not happen by federal edict, "high-quality teacher" guidelines, or hours of in-service. As Michael Fullan (2001) writes, schools change when teachers change their thinking: "it's as simple and complex as that" (p. 36).

The moments that shaped my teaching career are still clear landmarks in my mind. The time at the pond, described in Chapter 2, when my students became immersed in authentic scientific inquiry taught me about stepping back and making space for the questions. Another moment was at a restaurant—albeit a fast-food joint—where I stopped with a busload of middle-schoolers for supper after a long day outside in the field. I remember feeling so warmed by their lively chatter and happy interactions. I was grateful we were out in the "real world." Another moment was watching 12-year-olds hang on every word as they listened to a 90-year-old bird carver describe his work. I was struck by how many ways they could learn from others and that sometimes it happened in a very slow, concentrated way. Or there was the time I was asked by a seventh-grader if she could research a potato chip factory for her research project. "Potato chips?" I asked. I didn't have any reference point for this question. Her research was outstanding—interviews, diagrams of the process of potato to finished product, analysis of ingredients, and a brilliant summary of the economics involved. This was my lesson in being surprised.

What fed my determination to follow these moments was a hum that I could feel, a palpable buzz of learning together, wondering, and doing things that were worthwhile. The balance was tilted more to their learning and what they wanted to know than my teaching and what I wanted them to learn. This feeling was not present all the time, but it gave me inspiration for making decisions differently and helped me maneuver the many mandates that came my way. As teachers pursue new modes of teaching and learning, they make many choices about the structure and content of each minute of each school day.

Witnessing the complexity of these choices has been one of the most intriguing aspects of my work. One teacher described it as a "constant internal professional dialogue about all these connections." The reframing and implementation of this more authentic experience is an iterative cycle of learning that is prompted by the student engaging his world in new ways and demonstrating the value of that engagement to himself and the teacher.

"I'm doing things I never would have dreamed of doing 15 years ago."

Changing daily practice is a long process of re-orienting the work of the classroom toward a new purpose. It takes a long time. It is about small steps. A teacher doesn't sit down with her plan book in July and decide that by the following spring all her students will be fully engaged in changing the world. However, teachers, on their own, in small groups, or as part of whole-school initiatives, can engage in forward motion.

Traditional programs of professional development and school change initiatives have been built on a series of misconceptions about teaching and learning. The most blatant being that students and teachers learn when told, and that when told, their thinking changes. The view that teachers can be told how to teach is problematic for many reasons but particularly so when applied to local investigations. There are so many aspects to learning authentically in communities; a teacher's path to learning "how" varies. Most often, one best practice acts as a "carrier" for another and inspires the teacher to try something differently.

A teacher might be interested in service learning and witness the power of multi-generational relationships, so she might find ways to structure more of her language arts curriculum around interviews. Another might be studying a flood-plain and realize her students were more interested in cleaning it up than the plants growing there, so she might find more reasons to have science investigations serve a social need. Each teacher responds differently to the new possibilities given her skills, her beliefs, her training, her students, the nature of her particular workplace, and the community in which it sits. It is not one way, nor does it develop from one practice or appear as one strategy; it is a melding of many different decisions—for many different reasons.

Rethinking Professional Learning Experiences

Professional development should be devoted to teachers having time to learn the content in new ways and consider how to teach it to their students. Professional development can be built around the same rich tasks teachers want for their students. In order to understand the many skills involved in interviews, teachers should have the opportunity to interview others. In order to understand the power of concentration needed to draw outside, teachers should have the opportunity to spend time keeping a science or writing journal. To understand the thrill of planting a seed in newly tilled soil, teachers should have the opportunity to work in a garden. To feel the joy of creating something of value with others, teachers should have the opportunity to work together on meaningful projects. Teachers need time to ask questions, learn and do new things, explore new places, collaborate with peers, and share their new learning with others.

> "It is hard to correct one's own ineffective patterns if there is no true dialogue, collaboration, or reawakening of the student-like mind."
>
> Angela B. Peery (2004, p. 37)

Salvatore Vascellaro, in his book *Out of the Classroom and into the World* (2011), shares the legacy of Lucy Sprague Mitchell as a backdrop to a rich discussion of professional development and experiential learning. Mitchell, who founded and taught at Bank Street's school for teachers from 1930 through the early 1950s, took aspiring teachers on "Long Trips" to places where they could witness the setting for complex issues such as civil rights, coal mining, and rural and urban development. She would have them explore New York City through a number of different themes such as "Houses," "Roads," and "Food." One of her frequently used strategies was to ask teachers to first learn kinesthetically. On a busy street in Manhattan, she would ask them to stand on a corner, observe a road for five minutes with their eyes closed, and then use those impressions to write about what interested them. Her goal, reflected by one of her students years later, was to have us "listen the way a child would" (p. 89).

Vascellero brings to life many of Mitchell's practices in the classes he teaches (both at the graduate level and reflections on his own elementary classroom) and through his work with other teachers as they explore ways to *engage the local*. His descriptions of new teachers facing the challenge of learning outside of school provides a powerful narrative of how deep learning can affect their ability to bring about the same for their students. One of his graduate students drew these pipes:

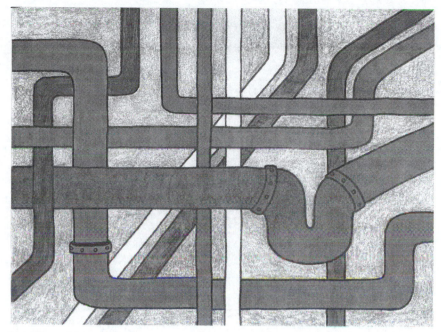

Mary Ellen Calabrese. Used with permisson.

I have had many wonderful experiences with teachers as they discover the learning possibilities that are, sometimes literally, in their backyard. Paddling a swamp near a school in northern Vermont, a teacher exclaimed: "I drive past here every day but have never explored. I can't wait to bring my students here. There is so much to learn." After visiting the local food shelf as part of a graduate class, a new teacher reflected: "There are so many things outside of school that students need to learn about. I want to bring my students here." Another teacher, after exploring the habitat behind the school, said: "There is a whole world happening out there that we didn't know about." A pre-service teacher explored an urban setting with a video camera and made a digital collage of doorways. It brought a new perspective to our view of the neighborhood—and the different doors told so many stories! "I never noticed them before," she said. Rethinking professional development involves teachers partaking in authentic learning experiences relevant to *their* personal experience, place, and possibilities.

When teachers experience the feeling of inquiry, the discomfort at having to chart a course, and the challenge of determining for oneself what is worthwhile, they will be much more capable of facilitating it for their students. To learn about how inquiry works, teachers need time to follow the questions.

The following template (Figure 9.1) is an experiential approach to professional development that introduces teachers to the fundamental aspects of local learning. It serves as a prompt for teachers to think about the four elements (See Part II) in the context of a specific place. It can be used to introduce teachers to

FOUR ELEMENTS AS PROFESSIONAL DEVELOPMENT	
FIND A QUIET PLACE TO SIT	**FIND A PLACE THAT CONNECTS TO ONE or more OF THE STANDARDS**
Consider the scale of the place you would like to observe. A vista looking out a great distance? A square foot of ground? A corner of the garden? Observe/write/draw what is happening in this place. You may be recording as an artist, a scientist… or a phrenologist! How does this place make you feel?	*(see sub-table below)* What evidence do you see that this concept is true? How does this BIG IDEA work in this place? What questions do you have?
What could your students learn and do here?	*How could your students use **one spot** to better understand one aspect of a BIG IDEA.*
THINK ABOUT THE MANY STORIES OF THIS PLACE	**CONSIDER OPPORTUNITIES FOR CIVIC ENGAGEMENT**
What is unique about this place? What evidence do you see of a human story? An animal story? An ecology story? What indications are there in this place of any hidden or untold stories?	What problems exist in this place? What evidence is there that people are/or are not working to solve them? What sources will help you understand some of the issues associated with this place?
What do you think the compelling story of this site would be for your students? How might you introduce them to this story?	*What problems might your students want to address? How might you get them interested in one of these issues?*

SUSTAINABLE DESIGN	CHANGE OVER TIME	PERSONAL EXPRESSION
HUMAN IMPACT	WEATHER	WATER CYCLE

FIGURE 9.1

Amy B. Demarest, Place-based Curriculum Design: Exceeding Standards through Local Investigations. © Routledge, 2015.

the fundamental considerations of local investigations or to deepen practice if place-based studies are already underway. Questions can be tailored to align with a specific place. Such intellectual considerations need to done alongside the time for teachers to explore, reflect, and discuss their findings with each other.

We often spend time with teachers outside discussing local phenomenon and finding the big ideas in the local landscape. Teachers stand next to a stratified rock and discuss an "earth moving" standard. They examine a transportation route with a city planner and discuss a big idea of economics such as the moving of goods and services or break open parts to a flower and discuss "life cycle." Professional development needs to provide these moments of close interaction with the real thing—otherwise teachers won't feel confident figuring out how to give their students these same opportunities.

Schoolwide Support of Local Learning

"Many principals have a crick in their neck because they're always looking up to see what's falling down on them from the powers above. In many cases, administrators have lost touch with a way to look out and see what powerful resources they have in their students and citizens. If they could see these things, it would change the whole life of the school."

Jack Shelton (2006, p. 8)

Schools can better support the complex process of teaching and learning in the context of community. Professional learning communities, community dialogue, and time to learn and plan for new things are all ways schools can organize around these complex interactions. Such a commitment reflects a change in school culture. It is hard to change old patterns. A pre-service teacher talking about how challenging it would be to change the way things were said: "*I am starting to see that it is not about being perfect but learning how to change when necessary.*" There are many things that support the work of changing—the most important of which is a culture of learning. A teacher presenting at a workshop with her colleagues commented: "*We've come to understand that change is a messy process. We know that there will be times that we disagree and it will be bumpy. But we are moving forward.*"

"The most powerful strategy for improving both teaching and learning is to create the collaborative culture and collective responsibility of a professional learning community."

Rick Dufour & Mike Mattos (2013, p. 37)

Professional dialogue that is supported by the structure and culture of the school can offer valuable opportunities for teachers to examine the logistics of *engaging the local.* Critical conversations about the role of school, the value of certain kinds of student work, and the implications of data are central to changing practice and changing schools. Teachers need time to learn how to make connections between how they think they should teach and how they want to teach. One teacher commented that her growing comfort with using local questions rested on the feeling that she was "permitted" to do this kind of teaching.

I used to think I wasn't allowed to do this. [Where I was trained] they don't even talk about this whole world and ways we have access to it as a teacher. . . . Teachers should know how to do this.

Professional Learning Communities (www.schoolreforminitiative.org) are life-lines for generating new energy in schools. Sandwiched into the small nooks and crannies of the school calendar, they provide islands of clarity in a teacher's busy life. Teachers meet and share their ideas, reflect on things they tried, review student work, and get feedback from colleagues in a safe, productive, forward-looking setting. Such gatherings provide support and concrete strategies for changing old patterns.

How Leadership Supports Change

While the main work of moving forward toward the deeper learning rests with teach-ers, the role of leadership is critical. Furman and Gruenewald (2004) say that school leaders need to "negotiate the borders and ideological dissonance between [conflict-ing messages]". First among their suggestions to resolve this discord is to "support teachers in their role as curriculum planners" (p. 70). They suggest leaders gain " . . . *a new language of possibility* . . . to redefine the meaning of accountability and assessment and to direct these educational tools to the social and ecological well-being of community life in and outside of schools" (p. 63). Aligning the school discourse on accountability with *a new language* involves rethinking what work is important and being able to articulate it clearly in the school and larger community.

Sometimes leadership can foster new thinking. One school principal (Moran, 2007) supports teachers by saying, "Tell me something of value that you want to teach about this community and I will give you a standard and a way to connect to content or tell me a standard and I will find a way to connect to the rich heri-tage and culture of this community." Daniel Feigelson, a literacy consultant with the New York City schools wished that more principals would adopt programs similar to Mrs. Krings's trip to the parking garage that is described in Chapter 7. He cited the pressure to perform well on tests as the perceived obstacles indicating that higher scores would not happen immediately. To commit to this kind of pro-gram, Feigelson commented: "[Y]ou'd have to be willing to take the long view" (Winerip, 2012, p. A16).

Taking the long view means many different levels of commitment from leader-ship. I recently worked in a school with a new principal. The teachers—who wanted to get their students outside more and use the land behind their school as a learning lab—were savoring the building-wide support and new enthusiasm for this work. They frequently mentioned the principal's encouragement, the work she had done to gather support from the school board and their appreciation of a long-range plan. To date, that support had not cost the school any great sum of money. However, the consistent voicing of positive support meant a great deal to the teachers as they were trying to change the course of their school.

Of course, the work takes more than vocal support. Fundamental changes in curriculum involve significant shifts in budgets, schedules, staffing, and materials. Schools need leadership that can effectively develop the synergy among commu-nity partners, classrooms, and the community to keep the vision front and center.

Smith and Sobel (2010) use an apt analogy when they liken the role of leadership to tending a garden:

> Because deep-seated curricular and instructional changes entail a transformation of fundamental aspects of a school culture, it is important for school leaders to see themselves more as gardeners than engineers. They can prepare the soil, make sure there is plenty of water, and put new starts in the ground after the danger of frost has passes, but they can't make the plants grow.
>
> *(p. 119)*

Tom Horn, former principal of the Al Kennedy School in Cottage Grove, Oregon, saw part of his job as cultivating partnerships with the community (Smith, 2011). As a result, students worked with the municipality in wetlands restoration projects and management of invasive species, took part in conversations and solutions to local housing issues, worked on community gardens, and worked in partnership with the US Forest Service in local forest restoration efforts. Horn believes that in addition to fostering these partnerships it was his job to keep the students' work visible (i.e., sharing information regularly with the school board, parents, other educators, and the general public).

School change builds the leadership capacity of *all* the people in the school's community. Such a vision comes alive in interactions with parents, on the website, in social media updates and public postings, on assessment tools, and in the work that students do. Leaders need to find ways to broadcast the mission not only to the public but throughout every inch of the school day. Brian Williams, principal of the Sustainability Academy in Burlington, Vermont (http://sa.bsdvt.org), states on the school's website: "I firmly believe in the power of education to create a future where social equity, environmental stewardship and economic equity are the norm and not the exception." Williams hosts a Monday morning community "town meeting," which a number of parents and community members attend. This is time to celebrate the accomplishment of the students, share student work, and remind students of their responsibility in and around the school. Williams encourages them for the upcoming week: "You are working so hard to learn important things and we are working so hard to teach you." Williams later explained (personal communication, November 29, 2013) that it was this transparency that he believed was essential to changing the climate of the school. "We hold each other accountable. It's all about relationships. If the student feels I have his back then we can do things. Without that, nothing works."

Carrie Brennan, principal of City High School, believes that one of leadership's main responsibilities is to sustain the relationships that teachers create in the community. She says:

> It is important to keep in mind that there is a continuum of involvement from the community that is sometimes very intense—like an artist's month-long residency or a one-time event when someone comes in to speak to a

class. Any one person or agency can move along that spectrum . . . there is some natural ebb and flow to their involvement. Funding may run out, a project may finish, or other commitments may get in their way . . . but they will come back. Part of my job is to maintain those relationships so they will still be connected to our work. Those people are the extension of your campus and the source of your support in the community. The next time you work with them it might look different.

(personal communication, November 27, 2013)

"Let the community be the teachers!"

Carrie sees another part of her role is to support alterations in the school day. This happens in large and small ways as City High School students interact with the community. City High School hosts a "Community Day" once a month when they suspend the regular schedule. Carrie describes it as time to "push the pause button on business as usual and dive into our mission." Suspending the schedule—even for that short a time—has a "huge influence on our relations with the community." There are different things scheduled; community partners present the programming. Students may spend time at a community farm or in a social service agency; it might be a career day or their annual school-wide retreat. Teachers learn alongside their students. Often the connections made during this day lead to a service project or internship at some future date (personal communication, November 27, 2013).

School change involves building a cohesive, visible, seamless, and sustained vision that keeps a school moving forward. All parts need to be working together. While leadership is critical, what happens each day for the students remains in the hands of teachers.

Challenges of Changing Practice

The energy and logistics, opinions and cooperation of other colleagues, and the structure of the school day—so many things affect a teacher's ability to change how learning happens. These challenges are felt on many levels. For example, getting your students out of the school building, a topic addressed more thoroughly in Chapter 7, is one of the more challenging aspects of local learning. Some of the challenges appear obvious, such the lack of money for buses or time in the schedule. Other challenges can come from external pressures such as the expectation to stay inside and get ready for tests. Other challenges are more personal, such as a teacher who says: "This is different from the way I am used to teaching; why focus so much on the local?"

The deeper obstacles are embedded in how teachers feel. If a teacher feels demoralized by the many demands on her time, getting kids out just seems like too much work. Whenever I hear teachers voice their frustration about the challenges of this style of teaching, we end up talking about forward motion. It is hard to change everything all at once—but going forward is about taking small steps in ways that can be uplifting.

Some teachers, by nature, may be less comfortable with inquiry. They may appreciate the role of questions but not want to devote so much time to the framing and the following of questions. The whole idea of investigations, the process of "handing it over," and working with unidentified sources and unknown answers may seem daunting. While it is helpful to keep in mind that conducting local investigations need not be about inquiry all day long, it can feel that way at the start. Teachers should do what they are comfortable with. There are many ways to *engage the local*.

Some teachers feel isolated when they are challenged to try something new. It can feel as if you are the only person in your school who believes in this kind of teaching. Sometimes that is the case. However, oftentimes, it is fruitful to begin a new collaboration or ask help for trying a new strategy. If need be, finding a colleague online or in another school can provide support and inspiration. When I started teaching about Lake Champlain, my most valued colleague taught seventh grade in another school. We planned lessons together that we taught to different students and took long walks after school with our dogs talking about the many challenges of field trips, reading, resources, and group dynamics.

Finally, there is a pervasive frustration with the "revolving door" of profes-sional development. Such an attitude is summed up by a teacher who says in response to a new directive: "Wait a minute. It will go away." Another teacher might rightfully say: "I have been doing project-based learning for years. Most of what my students do is grounded in the local community. Is this place-based inquiry? Why do people keep changing the names of things?" This criticism is justified. Some of my very favorite books about local investigations (see the online resource for more information: www.routledge.com/9781138013469) never mention the term place-based education. This can cause confusion when we try to communicate our intentions, but it is part of the educational world. Professional dialogue gives teachers tools to examine new practices and align new directives with the things that they know work—by whatever name they are called.

Strategies for Moving Forward

I have many conversations with teachers about the challenges of place-based edu-cation and how overwhelming it sometimes feels. Early on in the process, it often seems like too big a change involving practices that they either feel unprepared for or feel their colleagues and communities don't understand. Conversations about these obstacles invariably end up on the one strategy that seems to make sense. Just go forward. Make small changes.

A teacher who never assigns a piece of writing if he will be the only reader, reports how he started with one assignment. A teacher who routinely takes stu-dents on the city buses to spend time in the downtown area began with one bus trip. A teacher who now routinely matches students to community mentors so they can shadow the use of mathematics in the workplace started with one such partnership.

Expand the audience of the work that you assign. Add an interview as a required assignment to a research project. Go outside to draw. Invite a community member to come to talk to your class about fixing cars, growing food, driving a snowplow, or cleaning up a watershed. There are so many people who will will-ingly share their expertise. Try something. No matter how small. It will feed you. It doesn't have to mean that your students are going to change the world right away. Just start. Your students will show you the way.

"Second-graders, old folks, and purple beans . . . what could be bad?"

Many teachers express an enthusiasm for a "just try it" approach to professional learning. It is the courage to "jump in" that characterizes the forward motion. My colleague Katie Wyndorf offers these 10 tips that illustrate one teacher's personal credo of forward motion:

- Start early. Plan with some of the same considerations you would for any well-designed learning experience. Consider ways to provide in-depth and rich front-loading with a variety of materials and time for valuable reflection and closure.
- Do not romanticize a "place" for students. Instead, provide the platform for inquiry and allow students to unpack their connections, understandings, perspectives, and knowledge of place.
- Forge partnerships with community organizations/members. Connecting students with community members, whether as an additional guide/resource for the unit or as an authentic audience to showcase learning, is beneficial for all.
- Consider the logistics before leaving the classroom (i.e., medical needs, groupings, permission slips, etc.). Treat any place-based class outside of school the way you would if you were taking students on a hike or out on a field trip.
- Be sure to cover all your bases and get permission when necessary to implement service projects. Do this as early as possible. The world outside of school sometimes operates on a different time schedule.
- Look for ways to include content areas. Examining "place" lends itself to real-world learning—which is naturally interdisciplinary.
- Conduct your own personal research to find out more information about a place. Even if the enduring understanding or essential questions have not been solidified, it is important to gain as much insight into a place as possible, especially if the community that you work in is not the community that you live in.
- Remember that "place" does not necessarily need to be off campus. It is possible to facilitate a meaningful place-based inquiry on the school grounds. Also, "place" should not be confined to the natural environment.
- Do your best to ensure that all students see that they have made an impact, whether small or large, in their "place."
- Be fearless; do not be afraid to take risks.

Carve Out Time for New Learning

Although school schedules pose immense challenges to creating a forward-thinking learning community, teachers need the following:

- **Time to Talk.** Teachers, like all learners, need the time to make sense of their practice. Like all learners, they do not learn (only) in isolation, they do not learn (only) from reading, and they rarely learn from following directions. They learn when they can explore new ideas, consider what it means to their students, and have time to practice new skills and apply them in the real world.

- **Time to Plan.** The structure of a teacher's day should accommodate the job she needs to complete. This includes teaching and being with her students, planning what will happen during that time, doing the research and collaboration with other teachers and community partners, and completing the abundance of clerical work, phone calls/emails/posting to class websites, and data entry essential to her day-to-day job.

- **Time to Think and Reflect.** Teachers need time to ask, What does this mean to me? One of the great failures of school reform is how routinely teachers are thrown new initiatives with no time to process them. Some great ideas arrive at schools (or lay hidden on the shelf), and teachers aren't given time to strategize about their worth and feasibility. It's the teachers who decide how new initiatives are going to work, and they need time to consider the implications of the proposed change.

- **Time to Learn New Things.** Teachers need to spend time doing the things they are going to ask their students to do. They need to experience asking questions, finding answers, and learning new skills in local places. This does not mean time to learn about learning . . . but to be the actual learner. Teachers need time to experience places, do new things with people, and learn in different environments. In the river, on the subway, in the market, or the garden . . . in the field is where teachers can come to new understanding about what it means to learn outside of the classroom.

Listen to Students

When teachers are stumped about how to redesign a task, the simplest solution is to talk with students about what they think will work best. Ask students how they would like to accomplish an assessment. Ask questions about any assignments and ideas that you are trying to figure out. Share plans with them. Create plans with them. They are your best allies!

> "We educators and educational researchers must seriously question the assumption that we know more than the young people of today about how they learn or what they need to learn in preparation for the days ahead."
>
> Allison Cook-Sather (2002, p. 3)

A teacher designing a unit on alternative energy might hold a discussion that serves as a "needs assessment" to design a learning plan. She can ask students what they know, what terms are familiar, and what questions they have. Although this might be interpreted as a traditional "pre-assessment" to improve content acquisition, the act of holding a dialogue with students means that they can share and build on each other's ideas and become part of the process.

In Vermont, an organization exists that fosters this kind of dialogue between teachers and students. The mission of "UP for Learning" or Unleashing the Power of Partnership for Learning (www.upforlearning.com) is to: "Increase student engagement by developing youth-adult partnership in learning to ensure that each and every student has the skills, self-confidence and opportunities to assume meaningful roles in shaping their learning and their lives."

In their signature program, "Youth and Adults Transforming Schools Together" (YATST; www.yatst.com), high school youth-adult teams collect data from all students and teachers in their school about the level of relevance, relationships, rigor, and shared responsibility in their classrooms. Students then lead meetings to create a new shared language and norms to foster communication. A student reflected, "The student-led faculty meeting was unlike anything I have ever seen in terms of students and teachers holding a discussion about a topic as sensitive as their teaching methods. I heard from a lot of teachers in the 'go-around' that they were awestruck about what had just happened."

One question schools typically ask on the teacher survey is, "I check in regularly with students regarding their learning and adapt instruction accordingly." The parallel student question is, "Teachers check in regularly with me regarding my learning and adapt instruction accordingly." In virtually all schools, a "puzzling gap" emerged, with more than 90 percent of teachers reporting frequent check-ins, while one-third to one-half of students perceived that this was the case. Importantly, the results of the survey are discussed with students, and classroom strategies are adjusted to better address student needs.

"My uncle works on the ferry. Can he come talk to us about diesel engines?"

Often teachers discover a wealth of community resources and potential partnerships in these discussions. "Oh—I live near this old stone building that I think used to be used to generate power from the stream. I think my uncle knows someone who worked there." Or "My grandmother said that our school used to be in that building downtown next to the grocery store they are talking about tearing down. She went there until fifth grade and tells some great stories."

It is an immensely simple and profound practice to invite students in to the planning process. They have so much to say about how they can best learn, what connections are important to them, and how they can demonstrate their learning. Such reflection fuels their own learning and the learning climate of the school.

Take your students outside and watch them learn. They will teach you a lot about how to have an authentic experience. Follow the questions.

Create time in your classroom to discuss the why of what you are doing. Work to establish a clear purpose. You can't share an understanding of a goal unless everyone knows what it is. Explore the power of shared purpose.

Praksah Patel Photography. Used with permission.

Follow the Work

Pay attention to student work. When the work is redefined and investigations lead to a new kind of work, you and your students can figure out what they need to know in order to accomplish it. This is the sweet honey!

Where will you find this work? Not sitting on a shelf. Not tightly bound in a frame. A student-created neighborhood guide might be online, or people might be using it in the field to find out more about amphibian health or street redesign or rain gardens. It might be a meal shared with elders or the opening of a local history museum that is housed in a refurbished building with solar panels on the roof. The work is big and bold and useful. Indeed, some of it might be bound in a book cover . . . and available in the local library or being read by fourth-graders. Or it might be in an artist's frame and hung in the local shelter or community meeting room.

Develop authentic assessments that count as official measures of learning. Make the work public: murals, historical markers, radio spots, story signage, art in public spaces . . . so many possibilities. Create together what a vision of excellence would look like. The quality of the final work is not something that can be mandated but grows as the community is involved in the process. The elements might be set out in standards document, but the creative process of melding standards, young learners, and their communities is uncharted.

Assess the things that you value. Traditional assessment of knowledge and skills will always be part of a teacher's job. What is new is that a teacher can use the same rubric that provides feedback on the "regular" accomplishments to assess the deeper thinking and changes of attitude that drive this work. Students change their view of themselves and their communities when we enlarge the scope of the tasks we assign.

In order to be clear about these assessments, teachers need time to identify what is valuable to them, their students, and the community. This happens when the tasks are designed in partnership with others.

Reach Out to the Community

Share great work. Showcase student work in school; pursue public avenues for sharing new learning. Design work that is authentic and public. When the work is shared publicly—*something else happens.* The work generates new understanding and commitment. Assessment can come to be thought of as part of a process, not just a documentation of final understanding.

Identify the partners who will help you share student work. Student work that hangs on a wall can be displayed in banks, hospitals, and homeless shelters. Work that educates can be in grocery stores, subways, train stations, and parks. Signage can be a final project that teaches others about plants, buildings, sustainable practices, and recycling. Pursue new partnerships—creative alliances such as teaching gardens in prisons, schooling for teenage mothers in an old-age home, identifying service organizations that need youthful visionaries and problem-solvers, preschoolers that need stories with beautiful pictures and someone to read them, or shop classes that build houses for people that need them. The phrase "a democratic public education for all" has yet to be realized. There are so many untapped partnerships yet to be explored.

Celebrations are central to sharing work with the community. The more schools make public the new kinds of student work generated through local investigations, the more we can share new definitions of excellence and academic success.

★★★★★★★★★★

Engaging the local presents a spectrum of purpose that weaves together, in whatever ways teachers and students create the tapestry, the acquisition of content, practicing of authentic skills, and a chance to experience one's personal strengths and possible futures. Teachers come to see that education can be about solving problems, thinking critically, finding one's place in the world, and being part of solutions. Teachers reorient their thinking to these larger purposes and reframe the work they do with students.

Planning learning experiences that incorporate authentic investigations is a complex business for teachers. It changes "business as usual" for themselves, their students, and the work that they do together. In order to follow the power of these real questions, teachers undertake a journey. It is not a change that teachers make overnight; it is a forward motion that teachers engage in as they explore their communities with their students and discover the amazing and sweet opportunities for learning and living in community.

The creation of curriculum to meet the diverse needs of students and communities becomes a fluid undertaking and brings life to what has become—in many places—a deadened exchange of information. When the students and community are engaged in generating knowledge, it becomes a more vibrant process. There is a hum, a convergence of purpose, self-direction, knowledge, and future possibilities.

"The big, deep experiences touch a kid's sense of purpose."

In the end, it comes down to a matter of the heart. Ellen reflects on *engaging the local:* "It's individually based . . . within the individual. This is the place," she said, touching her heart as she spoke. This is how we need to rest our definition of a worthy frame for curriculum design: on what the student makes of it and what he takes away. To make space for that meaning to gain traction remains the challenging task for the teacher as a designer of curriculum and as a human being.

★★★★★★★★★★

References

Cook-Sather, A. (2002). Authorizing students' perspectives: Toward trust, dialogue and change in education. *Educational Researcher, 31*(4), 3–14. http://dx.doi.org/10.3102/0013189X031004003

Dufour, R., & Mattos, M. (2013). How do principals really improve schools? *Educational Leadership, 70*(7), 34–40.

Fullan, M. (2001). *The new meaning of educational change.* New York, NY: Teachers College Press.

Furman, G., & Gruenewald, D. (2004). Expanding the landscape of social justice: A critical ecological analysis. *Educational Administration Quarterly, 40*(1), 47–76. http://dx.doi.org/10.1177/0013161X03259142

Moran, S. (2007, March). *Place-based education in the Northeast and beyond.* Presented during School Administrator's Panel at The 4th Promise of Place Conference, Fairlee, VT.

Peery, A. B. (2004). *Deep change: Professional development from inside out.* Lanham, MD: Scarecrow Education.

Shelton, J. (2006). Alabama silos: A conversation with Jack Shelton. *Democracy and Education, 16*(2), 6–9.

Smith, G. (2011). Linking place-based and sustainability education at Al Kennedy High School. *Children, Youth and Environments, 21*(1), 59–78.

Smith, G., & Sobel, D. (2010). *Place- and community-based education in schools.* New York, NY: Routledge.

Vascellaro, S. (2011). *Out of the classroom and into the world: Learning from field trips, educating from experience, and unlocking the potential of our students and teachers.* New York, NY: The New Press.

Winerip, M. (2012, February 12). A field trip to a strange new place: Second grade visits the parking garage. *The New York Times*, p. A16.

Zinn, H. (2006). *A power governments cannot suppress.* San Francisco, CA: City Lights.

INDEX

Lightning Source UK Ltd.
Milton Keynes UK
UKOW01f2140220915

259091UK00009BA/317/P